"As a girl, Jani Buron literally grew up with the legendary Seabiscuit at historic Ridgewood Ranch. She shares her story of life in this almost-forgotten era of California, studded with fascinating people and beautiful places. Her one-of-a-kind photos illustrate her fine storytelling. The result is a little gem that will be treasured, not only by racing fans, but anyone interested in Golden State history."

Debbie Arrington
Sacramento Bee turf writer

<<<<>>>>

"Jani Buron has painted us a thoughtful picture of what life was like at Ridgewood Ranch and the town of Willits during the time of Seabiscuit. The rich details she provides are unique to a special time and place. Rich in photos, charts and personal stories, she accurately portrays the Howard Family and the rustic 'out of the spotlight' world of Seabiscuit."

Col. Michael C. Howard, U. S. Marines
Great Grandson of C. S. Howard

<<<<>>>>

"What I most appreciate about Jani Buron's book, *The Spirit of Seabiscuit,* is that it so accurately captured the warmth and generosity of Marcela Howard, who so graciously welcomed me into the Howard Family when I married C. S. Howard's grandson, Lindsay Howard Jr. Jani's book is a labor of love."

Barbara Beck Howard
Author of *Letters To Seabiscuit*

<<<<>>>>

Laura Hillenbrand's exquisitely written best-seller book, *Seabiscuit; An American Legend,* brought the grandeur of Seabiscuit's racing career back to the American public. Ms. Hillenbrand's book recalled memories of my own life at Ridgewood Ranch in the 1940s, a time that I loved so much. I knew Seabiscuit and the Howards, and later the racetrack. It all inspired me to write the rest of the story and share it with you. Thank you, Laura.

Jani Buron
Author of *Ridgewood Ranch, Home of Seabiscuit* and *The Spirit of Seabiscuit*

<<<<<<<<<<<<<<<<<<<<>>>>>>>>>>>>>>>>>>>

*The early years ...*

THE PLEASANTON TIMES, PLEASANTON,
APRIL 22, 1954

# JAN GRIFFITH OUTSTANDING MEMBER OF AMADOR CSF

From Ridgewood Ranch near Willitts, California, came the Chet Griffith family to Pleasanton, shortly before their daughter Janet was to enter high school as a freshman in 1950. Jan has been one of the outstanding members of her class during the entire four years —outstanding because of her loyalty and devotion to the principles of fine school citizenship.

Janet's mother, Mrs. Inez Griffith, is well-known as a fourth-grade teacher in the Pleasanton Grammar School. There is a younger brother, to, who is in the fourth grade, but not in his mother's class.

At the Ridgewood Ranch Janet's father was a foreman of horses. One can see that Jan came by her interest in horses honestly, since her father's work has always been with them, and she first rode a horse before she could walk, at the tender age of eight months.

Janet will graduate this June as a straight college prep student. In this, her senior year, she is studying homemaking, typing, civics, drama, and English. In connection with her English work Janet has become deeply interested in writing, and her English composition shows warmth and thought. She won a certificate in the Alameda County Centennial Essay Contest last June and was third place winner in the Lions' Club Oratorical Contest of 1953.

A favorite hobby of Janet's is drawing and color art work. This talent equips her admirably for all sorts of decorating jobs around school. Her efforts in this direction resulted in a beautiful Junior Prom in 1953 under her able chairmanship.

Janet enjoys sports also and is a dependable player on all girls' teams. She is a member of Girls' Block A and has already won her G.A.A. pin.

In the spring of '53 Janet was chosen with three others of her class to attend the Girls' Leadership Conference at Asilomar. In

JAN GRIFFITH

the way of leadership during her senior year she has served her Student Body as it Parliamentarian and has sat on the Student Council. She is also active in dramatic activties and played the role of Mary Jones in the Senior play last November. Another of Jan's activities is the Spanish Club, of which group she served as president in the spring term of 1953. The Future Homemaker of America chapter at Amador finds her a valuable member also.

In personality Janet may be said to be both vivacious and steady, inspiring both merriment and confidence in her fellow students.

Janet's future plans are to attend the University of California at Davis, where she will train for either elementary school-teaching or for secondary work in the field of home economics. She says she'll always be studying English, too. Whatever Jan does, our affectionate wishes for success will accompany her, and we extend to her our heartfelt thanks for being a good companion throughout these wonderful high school years.

—By Elizabeth Snyder.

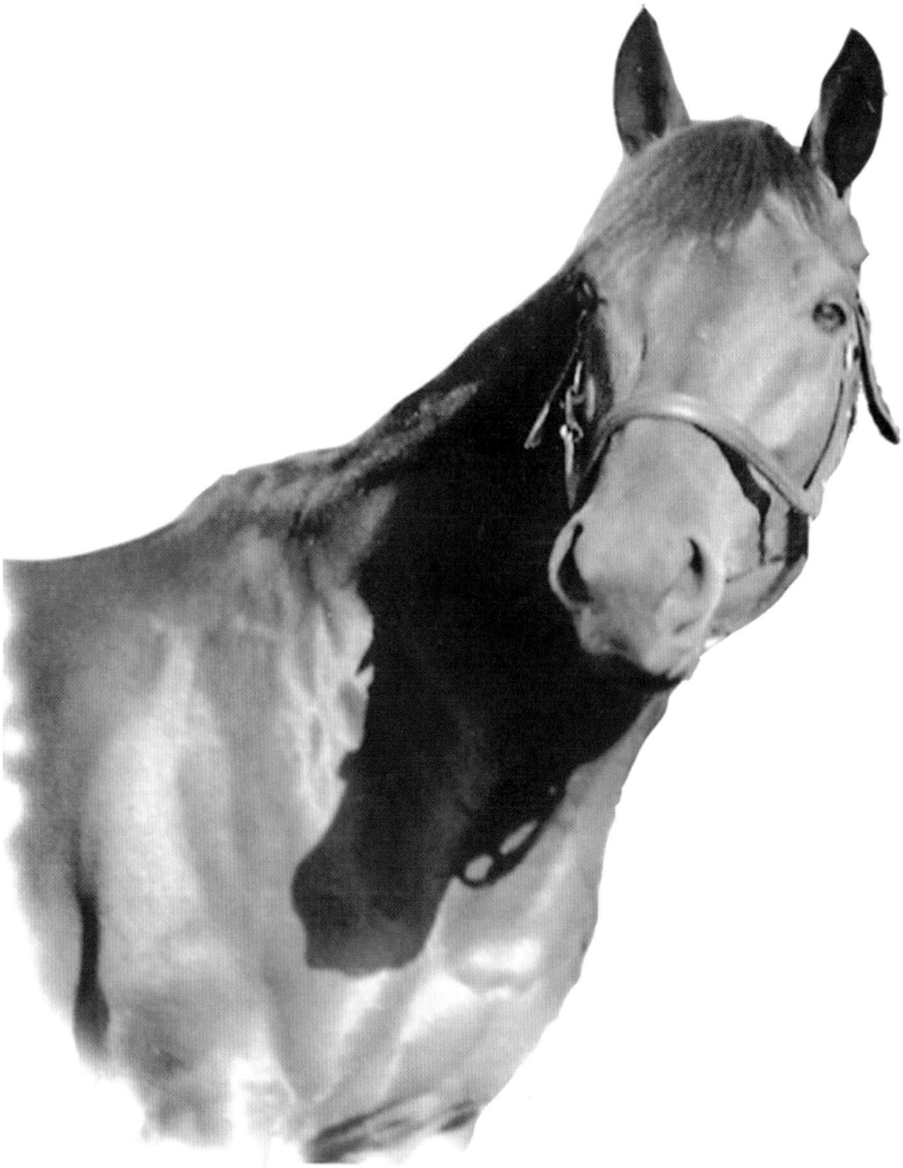

# The Spirit of Seabiscuit

# The Spirit
## of
# Seabiscuit

**Jani Buron**

L. L.Publishing
P.O. Box 12
Wellington, Nevada 89444

Financing sponsored by
Chris and Anita Lowe

Publisher's Cataloging-In-Publication Data
(Prepared by The Donohue Group, Inc.)

Buron, Jani (Janet)
The Spirit of Seabiscuit / [Jani Buron ; graphics and editing by L. Buron].

p. : ill., map ; cm.

Includes photo index.
ISBN-13: 978-0-9720755-2-7
ISBN-10: 0-9720755-2-6

1. Seabiscuit (Race horse) 2. Race horses—United States—Biography. 3. Horse racing—United States. 4. Ridgewood Ranch (Calif.)—History. 5. Howard, Charles Stewart. 6. Buron, Jani (Janet) I. Buron, L. II. Title.

SF355.S4 B87 2006
798.4/0092/9 2005902360

## About This Book

The information in this book is correct, to the best of my knowledge. History sometimes changes with the re-telling of it, so there may be facts in here that differ from the opinions of others who read it.

Research shows that this is the way it was, and my memory of being there recalls the years I lived it. My mission is to present an account of that time in an interesting fashion for the enjoyment of my readers I hope this has been accomplished.

There are volumes more to be written of the people and events in these accounts:
Watch for more stories about Rench Angle
Charles Howard, Doc Raymond Babcock, Tom Smith,
Samuel Riddle, John Pollard, George Woolf
Joe Ferguson, Hubert Jones, Tex Wheeler and
all the winners that surround the spirit of Seabiscuit.

# DEDICATION

To *The Spirit of Seabiscuit*, his great heart and determination;
To his remarkable 89 races with all the great accomplishments;
To all those that were connected to him, and all horsemen now;
To all his public, then and now, who follow his greatness forever.

Of Seabiscuit's two identical memorial statues, expertly crafted by Tex Wheeler, one is standing at Santa Anita Racetrack in Arcadia, California, and the other, that originally stood at Ridgewood Ranch, now stands at The National Museum of Racing and Hall of Fame at Saratoga, New York.

These words are on the base of each statue:

*"Biscuit's courage, honesty, and physical prowess definitely placed him among the Thoroughbred immortals of turf history. He had intelligence and understanding almost spiritual in quality."*

# TABLE OF CONTENTS

**Dear Reader** .................................................................... **13**
**Poem by Jani Buron " The Spirit of Seabiscuit "** ............................ **14**
**Foreword** .................................................................... **15**
**Old Map of Mendocino County, California** ................................ **19**
**Timeline, 200 Years Plus** .................................................... **20**
**Howard Family Children** .................................................... **43**

**Chapter 1 The Ridgewood Barn Builders** .................................... **59**
C. S. Howard purchase of Ridgewood, The Barn Builders, WW II, Seabiscuit's 1939 trip home to heal, Red Pollard at Ridgewood and Red's wedding, Seabiscuit's 1940 homecoming to retire, Seabiscuit's barn, The Elko Connection.

**Chapter 2 The First Time At Ridgewood** .................................... **77**
The first time Dad worked at Ridgewood, Living in Laytonville, WW II troops, Soldiers and Seabiscuit photos, Job change from Ridgewood to Willowbrook, Sherwood Valley, Doc Babcock, New Brother, Forest Fire, Jones girls and music lessons, Horse van adventure on the bridge, Dad's racehorse Willow Count, Sherwood school, End of school year and Summertime.

**Chapter 3 Return to Ridgewood** .............................................. **93**
Living with the Jones family, Mr. Howard's offer of new house, Dad's new position, Floyd Banker's Ukiah house, Late evening earthquake, Hubert, Trip to Pleasanton, The move to the cookhouse, Ride to Payne's place, Upper Mare Barn apartment, Buggy Horse Barn, Howard Hospital, Doc Babcock and John, Billy the Kid, The Polo Pony, Bucky the fawn.

**Chapter 4 Growing Up At Ridgewood** ........................................ **127**
New house done, Hen's nest, Lower Mare Barn and foals, Bucks in Billy's field.

**Chapter 5 The Stud Barn, and Seabiscuit at Home** ...................... **139**
The visitors that came to see Seabiscuit, Sarge, Biscuit's first Foals, The Bridge story, Mama Kitty and the Biscuit, Seabiscuit is gone, Statues at Santa Anita, Ridgewood, then Saratoga Springs, New York.

## TABLE OF CONTENTS
**( Continued )**

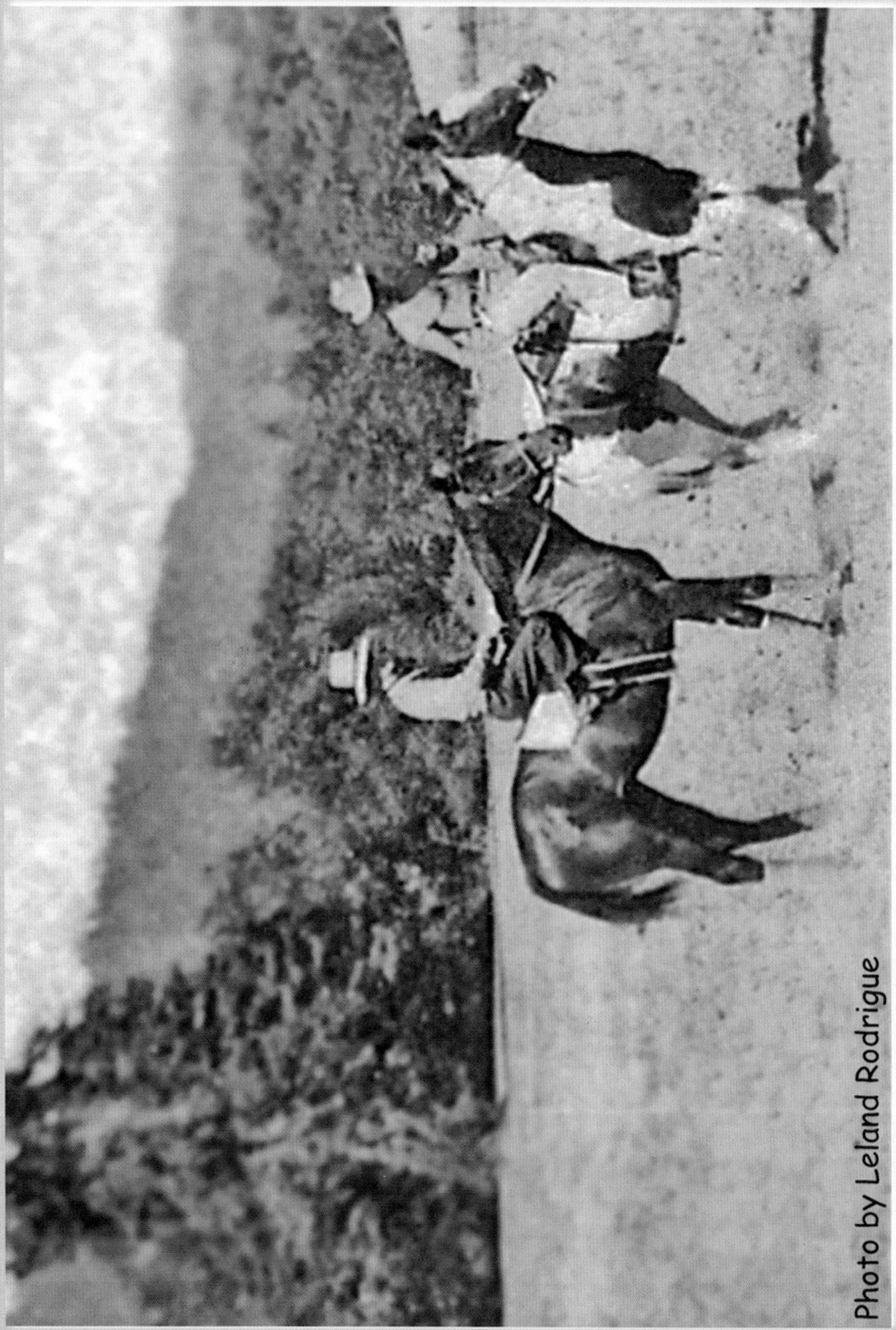

Seabiscuit with Red Pollard up in training at Ridgewood Ranch, led by Tick Tock, 1939

Photo by Leland Rodrigue

Dear Reader,

In this story you will find history and life on Ridgewood Ranch from the 1800's down through the Howard family early years with Fannie May and their four sons; then later, focusing on the Seabiscuit years with Marcela. In my first book *Ridgewood Ranch, Home of Seabiscuit* (2002) the story of Ridgewood was not as detailed as you will find it here. There will be references to a few similar stories, because Seabiscuit, Ridgewood, the Howards, and the community were all so intertwined; you cannot mention one without including the other.

In this book you will find rare and precious photos of life around Seabiscuit from private collections, some of which have not been previously published. Some of these photos are aged and therefore not perfect, but that lends to the flavor of the history being told. We can look upon the faces and surroundings and see how they lived. We have chosen to use these photos because they add to the meaning of the story.

This story contains some, but not all the statistics of Seabiscuit's fabulous career, nor does it describe the thrilling scenes of his wonderful racing days. This is the retired Seabiscuit we knew as children. We learned a lot more about his previous racetrack career later on, when we became grownups. We went on to the racetrack and became acquainted with horseracing, and raced our own horses, and it was then that we learned what it took to make a true champion like The 'Biscuit.

Retired at Ridgewood, Seabiscuit was a mellow horse, coming over to the fence to say hello and nuzzle us for carrots. The other studs were not so friendly; they came over to the fence with mischief in mind, tossing their head and they would rather nip than nuzzle. All the Howard stallions were handsome and shiny and well cared for, and it was a delight to watch them prancing around their paddocks showing off. But the 'Biscuit was relaxed and reachable, and he communicated with us, and we felt him reaching out to say "hello". The 'Biscuit was different, and anyone who was close to him knows that.

From the author,
Jani Buron

# The Spirit of Seabiscuit

Theme of a book of the same title

Racing hero, with a kind soulful eye
Do you know how much time has passed us by
Since you ran your races and thrilled your crowds,
Made happy people cheer and scream out loud
As you came down to the wire, lengths ahead,
Winning with class and speed,like most of'em said.
You became our favorite; and you are still
We treasure your spirit, and always will.

*Jani Buron*

# FOREWORD

Some places on this earth have a spiritual presence you become aware of when you enter their domain. You may notice a warm feeling in those surroundings. There was something so special about their lifetime that their greatness lingers on down through the ages. A true champion such as Seabiscuit, whose story has been told over and over, has such a presence on the land in the Walker Valley where he lived out his after-racing years. He lived here in a luxurious, oak tree shaded paddock within sight of the Howards' Ridgewood Ranch home. He received the best of care and attention. He sired a family of "Little Biscuits". He and Mr. Howard went on long rides together over the Ridgewood hills. Now Seabiscuit rests here eternally.

Some valleys have qualities that make them special forever. In Northern California, just inland from the Pacific Ocean, there is such a place named Walker Valley. By it's size, shape, location, and climate, it has a very unique appeal to many that have passed through it. Over the years, some saw it and went on, some stayed, and some came back to it. But none forgot it.

The Walker Valley is a pleasing variety of elevations, flat fields, gentle slopes, and rugged timbered hillsides, and is blessed with a good system of waterways running through it. Its climate is different from either valley that lies to the north or south of it, being more moderate than both. It seems like a paradise. And Paradise it was for some.

The earliest Native American Indians who lived in the Walker Valley recognized and appreciated the fine climate and abundant vegetation and plentiful water. Signs of their villages still remained when we were children there on the Ranch. We used to play our childhood games in the large saucer-shaped indentations in the ground that had served long before us as a base for their teepees. We found remnants of the hunting tools and food preparation objects of those who had lived there earlier.

The first white men to come through also regarded this valley as special, and some settled there and built homes and began planting crops and buying livestock. They made their living off the land, and raised their families here.

Around 1919 a man named Charles Howard began looking for the perfect location to build a working ranch and breeding farm that would fulfill his dream of owning a self-sufficient and self-supporting place, and also serve as a showcase for his fine Thoroughbreds. He wanted a true country place to call home for himself and his family.

He found the opportunity he was looking for in the Walker Valley, where a ranch that had become available looked like a good start toward what he envisioned. He purchased this large piece of ground. Then he began his plans to enlarge and improve on his new property in order to create his dream ranch.

Mr. Howard was a businessman, self-made, hard working, and always looking for new opportunities. He had excelled in many things, and was proud of his endeavors. One of his favorite projects was his Thoroughbred racing stable he had put together. He had many top-notch winners, and he enjoyed the sport of racing very much. He was a fine sportsman, and he enjoyed the challenge of the game.

His 1936 purchase of a then little known horse named Seabiscuit became another success for him. It seemed like destiny that the two should come together, and likewise for all the others close to Howard and this horse. When Seabiscuit was moved to the Howard racing stable, a legend was born, a legend about a racing career and a special horse, the men around him that would long outlive the lifetimes of those who created it.

In 1940, Charles Howard brought his now famous horse, Seabiscuit, to Ridgewood Ranch at the end of his racing career, after returning from injury and winning The Santa Anita Handicap on his third try. It was a great event for both of them. Seabiscuit was retired to stud at his new home located in the Walker Valley, just south of the small town of Willits, California.

Seabiscuit retired as the world's leading money winner of his day, with $437,730 to his credit. His five year racing record speaks for itself; out of 89 starts, he won 33 races, finished second 15 times and third 13 times. He was assigned far more weight than many of his competitors, but that didn't weigh The 'Biscuit's heart down. He ran on heart. His thrilling stretch runs proved that. He endeared himself to the racing public with his courageous dramatic finishes. The 28 races where he finished back in the field were mostly in his early racing years, before Mr. Howard bought him and gave him to Tom Smith to train and entrusted Red Pollard and George Woolf to ride him.

Even though Seabiscuit had known the excitement of racing and the rigors of being in training at the racetrack, he had a calm disposition about him at the Ranch, calm enough so that Mr. Howard and his wife Marcela, could enjoy riding him around the Ranch. Very few horses who race at the track make a good saddle horse for pleasure riding. Seabiscuit was one of the rare exceptions. Seabiscuit and Mr. Howard were very good pals. A racing champion, Seabiscuit set eleven new track records and equaled two!.

Now both are gone, yet who is to say where their spirits roam? So much of their wonderful life was lived out here in the beautiful countryside of this valley. So much still remains visible of how they lived, what they built, and of their accomplishments and their generosities. Those of us who shared that era and the excitement of those earlier times, remember. We are grateful to have been a part of them. The pictures we recall in our own memories are invisible to others, yet we can create word pictures of what we remember, and of what made it so special, and share the times past with present day followers of The Seabiscuit Story.

The Spirit of Seabiscuit lives on in the hearts of all who knew him then, and all who know of him now through the many new pictures and stories being retold. The fine example he set of giving his all, never quitting, even against all odds, and his intelligence and unique understanding of his world, will always be with us. The qualities that made him a true champion and hero gave us some examples to live by, and instilled the thought: "Yes, if Seabiscuit can do it, I can do it! I'll just try harder!"

Seabiscuit's spirit still roams the Ridgewood hills. He gallops easily and freely from the pristine meadows up to the hilltops to survey his Walker Valley home. He looks over the lush green pastures below where he spent the remainder of his enjoyable days after being retired from his racing career. In Horse Heaven, the ground is soft beneath his feet, the grass is tall and green, he drinks from sweetwater streams, and blue skies and warm days abound. Alfalfa fields dotted with apple trees and carrot patches are on the gourmet horse menu. Oak trees standing beside clear blue lakes and sparkling streams offer a cool place to take a nap on a summer day. Maybe there is even a little racetrack where he can show them how to run! What happier occupation is there than keeping company with your friends and galloping across these fields of Paradise!

These elegant words that Mr. Howard had inscribed on the base of Seabiscuit's statue describe this special horse with graceful simplicity:

*"Biscuit's courage, honesty, and physical prowess definitely placed him among the Thoroughbred immortals of turf history. He had intelligence and understanding almost spiritual in quality."*

Eagle Peak is a landmark that is seen from Ridgewood and surrounding areas

*Early Walker Valley History*

*Ridgewood Ranch*

*Howard Family*

*Seabiscuit*

*Present Day*

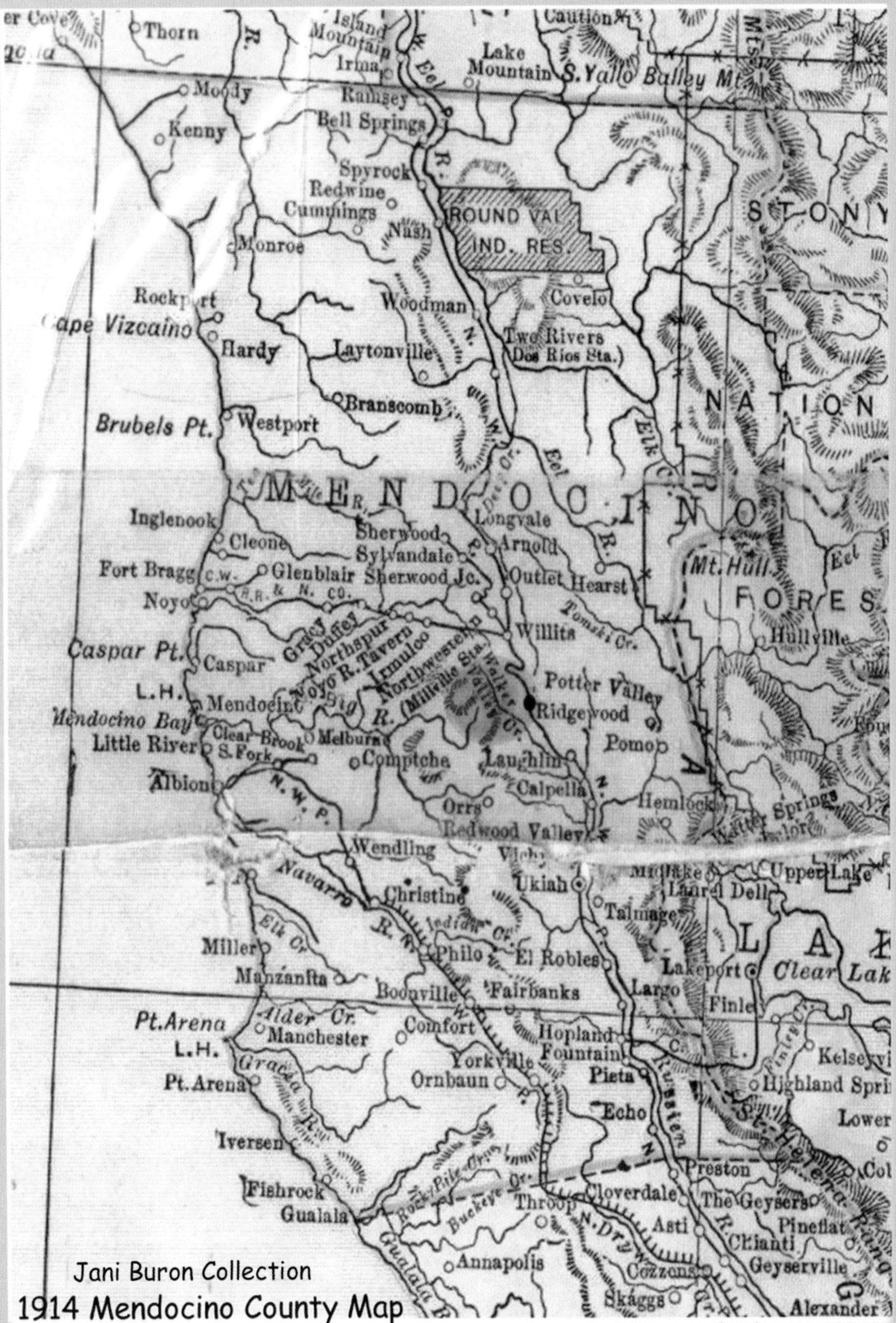


Jani Buron Collection

1914 Mendocino County Map

Walker Valley is marked in the center of the map

# TIMELINE, 200 YEARS PLUS

**1800's:** The Northern Pomo Native American Indians had camps in the Walker Valley, on the land that is now known as Ridgewood Ranch, in Northern California just south of Willits on Highway 101.

**1828:** Rench Angle, an early owner of the land now called Ridgewood Ranch, was born in Washington, Tazewell County, Illinois. He died in September of 1889 in Walker Valley, Mendocino County, California, and is buried in the Angle Family cemetery on Ridgewood Ranch.

**1840:** Mahulda Catherine Orender (the future Mrs. Rench Angle) was the third child born to her parents on November 7 in Warsaw, Hancock County, Illinois. She died on June 14, 1926 in Ukiah, Mendocino County, California.

**1850's:** Captain Walker had passed through this valley, and liked it so well that he brought his family back to it and built a home there. They were the first white settlers to stay in the Walker Valley. They farmed the land and raised cattle.

**1852:** During Rench Angle's long ownership of the land where Ridgewood now stands, he acquired many pieces of adjoining property. The place was called "Ranch Angle".

**1859:** Rench Angle, age 31, took Mahulda Catherine Orender, age 19, as his bride on June 7, in Sonoma County, California.

**1860:** Rench and Catherine Angle began their family. Altogether, they had a large family of 15 children, nine boys and six girls. Nine of the children died young. See further details of the Angle family history elsewhere in this book .

In 1878, six of Rench and Catherine's children died within fifteen days of each other when they contracted diphtheria from their domestic water well that became contaminated. According to a Granddaughter of the first Angle child, that 18 year old daughter, named Euphrasia Angle, helped her father bury all of her brothers and sisters lost in that tragedy. The small fenced and tree-shaded Angle Family cemetery is on a little rise in the middle of a field at Ridgewood, where it is tended to regularly.

**1875 to 1883:** The legendary Black Bart robbed stages from Sonora to Willits and from Weaverville to Downieville. The famous Black Bart Rock was located beside Highway 101,

Euphrasia, Rench, Annie and Catherine Angle

Martha Mitchell Collection

Euphrasia Angle, first child of 15 Angle children

a little south of the old main gate of Ridgewood Ranch .

**1877:** Charles Stewart Howard is born in the state of Georgia on February 28 to Robert Stewart Howard and Lucy Ellen Outram Howard.

**1880:** Fannie May Smith is born, the future Mrs. Charles Howard, the mother of his four sons.

**1889:** Mr. Rench Angle died September 2, at age 60, and was buried in the family cemetery on Ridgewood Ranch, where many of his children rest.

**1891:** The widowed Catherine Angle married Sylvester Drew on July 1, in Mendocino County, California.

**1900:** Mrs. Catherine Angle Drew, who had remarried, had to sell the "Ranch Angle", as the once large family fortune was now gone.

**1901:** Charles Stewart Howard married Fannie May Smith on Christmas Day, December 25, 1901, in East Orange, New Jersey. (The Howard family descendants page follows this timeline.)

**1902:** Charles Stewart Howard II was born in New Jersey, first son of C.S. Howard and Fannie May Howard.

**1903:** Charles Stewart Howard got out of the Army and boarded a train for San Francisco. His wife, Fannie May, and their first son stayed on the East Coast until such time as Charles got established and found a home for them out West.

**1903:** William Van Arsdale of San Francisco purchased the large piece of property south of Willits, California, in the Walker Valley, known today as Ridgewood Ranch. He raised cattle successfully. The previous owner, Rench Angle, had been a sheep rancher, and had done well with them.

**1903:** Marcela Zabala was born on September 22. She became Charles S. Howard's second wife, and together they owned a fine stable of Thoroughbred racehorses, including the famous Seabiscuit.

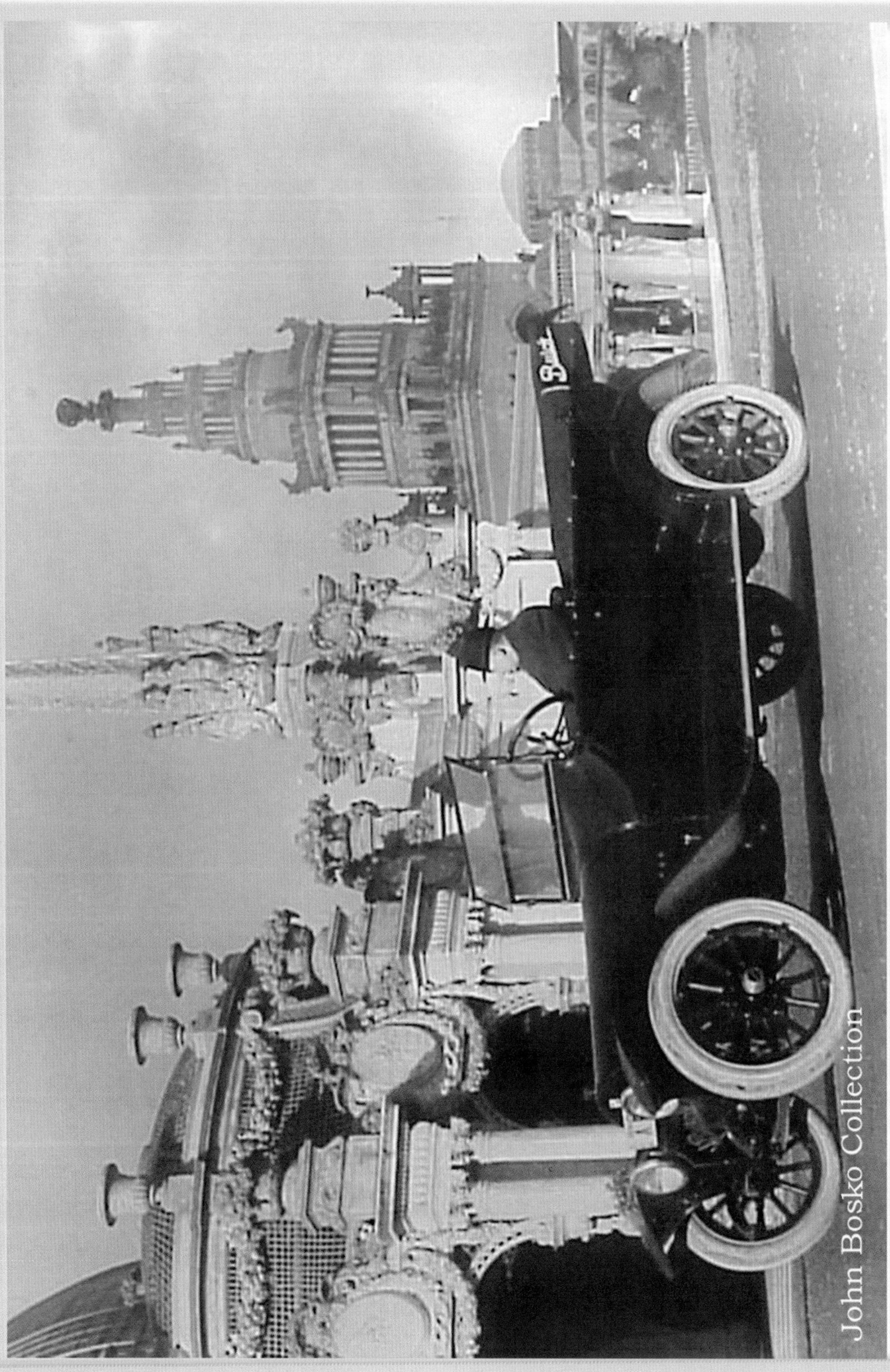


A Howard Buick in San Francisco during the early days of the automobile

**1904:** Lindsay Coleman Howard was born in New Jersey, second son of C.S. Howard and Fannie May Howard.

**1905:** The Van Arsdales built a large elaborate ranch house on a hill above the main ranch compound that had a commanding view of the ranch. The 1905 date is in cement above the mantle on the large outdoor stone fireplace in the patio, one of four such fireplaces in the home. This house was known as "The Big House" when the Howards owned the ranch later on. The house still stands today, to be enjoyed by the visitors to Ridgewood.

**1905:** Mr. Van Arsdale also developed a covered reservoir and water system on the east end of the property above the ranch where the plentiful springs are, piped water down to the ranch and used a Pelton water wheel to generate electricity. Although it is no longer used, the Pelton wheel is still on Ridgewood in the "light plant" house.

**1905:** C. S. Howard had been working at a job in San Francisco in a shop on Golden Gate Avenue, making and selling bicycles. He was intrigued with the invention of the automobile, and by 1905 he felt that it was the coming thing. He took a trip to Detroit, Michigan, to find out more about the industry. His enthusiasm and business know-how garnered him a Buick automobile distributorship for eight western states.

**1906:** In April the great San Francisco earthquake brought the city down, and the Howard Buick agency volunteered all the cars they had to help transport the injured to get medical help, and to take supplies wherever they were needed. The big Buicks could navigate over the wreckage quite well in some places, where horses couldn't go. People remembered this generous gesture.

**1906:** This year General Motors built 2,295 new Buicks, and the Howard Automobile agency had its share of cars to sell. Mr. Howard selected salesmen who knew their business, and paid good attention to advertising and publicity, and brought America's attention to the new mode of travelling, the automobile.

**1907:** C. S. Howard drove a two-cylinder Buick from San Francisco to Oakland, going through San Jose, and the trip took five hours to complete. This brought additional attention to the automobile, especially in the West, and stirred peoples' curiosity about the new motor car.

**1907:** On June 18, Catherine Angle married John Christy in Mendocino County, California.

John Bosko Collection

A Buick promotion in Virginia City, Nevada by the Howard Agency

**1910:** C. S. Howard began getting entire trainloads of new Buicks shipped to San Francisco, which became quite a curiosity to the locals. They lined the tracks to watch the new Buicks go by on their way to the Howard dealership, as many as 375 new cars on a train at one time in 1912. It was quite a sight in those days.

**1911:** Frank Robert Howard was born on October 15th, 1911, the third son of C.S. Howard and Fannie May Howard.

**1916:** Robert Stewart Howard, was born on April 21st, 1916, the fourth son of C. S. Howard and Fannie May Howard,

**1912 - 1913:** California was second only to New York in new car registrations, and one out of ten Buicks was sold through the Howard distributorship. Charles S. Howard moved his Buick showroom location to a spacious new 40,000 square foot four-story building on Van Ness Avenue at California Avenue. One of Mr. Howard's publicity stunts was to drive a parade of Buicks through Yosemite Valley. He was nearly arrested, because motor cars were not allowed there at that time, but the headlines he gained were great for Buick awareness! A few years later, Charles Howard was referred to as the world's largest motor car dealer in America. Another promotion that was not so risky was when they drove from Oakland, California to Reno and Virgnia City, Nevada

**1921:** C. S. Howard purchased Ridgewood Ranch in April. He soon began to expand and make improvements. This would be his new country estate, a place for his family to really call "home". It would become a place to raise his livestock, and to provide for his Thoroughbred horse breeding facility. He planned to make it his dream ranch of self-sufficiency, and a place to entertain his many friends who also enjoyed the country atmosphere and the fine horses. He succeeded in creating such a place, and everyone who lived and worked there enjoyed the benefits of his plan.

**1925:** The fact that the entrance to Ridgewood was located on the 101 Highway, almost equidistant between Willits and Ukiah, was of constant concern to each town's Chamber of Commerce. Each community wanted the claim to fame of being the home of Charles S. Howard's Ridgewood Ranch, and his famous horse, Seabiscuit. At some point, Mr. Howard had made it clear that Willits was the community that Ridgewood belonged to. Depending on what town a journalist was associated with, they wrote about Ridgewood as being "north of the town of Ukiah", or as being "south of the town of Willits".

**1926:** While C. S. and Fannie May Howard were away from Ridgewood for the weekend of May 8th and 9th, their third son, Frankie, and two of his friends, went for a morning

John Bosko Collection

For Buick publicity, Howard toured Yosemite Park in California

Jani Buron Collection

Home of Seabiscuit, Ridgewood Ranch Entry

David Bacci Collection

Frank R. Howard Memorial Hospital in 1934, in Willits, California

fishing outing on a Ridgewood stream. On the way back home, the truck overturned, and Frankie received fatal injuries. Help was summoned, but nothing could be done. There was no nearby medical facility that could have perhaps saved his life, and because of this, Mr. Howard saw to it that a hospital was built in the town of Willits to serve future medical needs of the community, in honor of the son he lost.

**1926-1927:** Planning and construction began on the Frank R. Howard Memorial Hospital, financially backed by Charles and Fannie May Howard in memory of their son Frankie. Doc Babcock oversaw the planning, and made suggestions for the new medical facility. In the traditional Howard style, only the best of building materials and the most modern equipment went into the hospital. Mr. Howard made plans to supply food, meat, and dairy products to the hospital from Ridgewood Ranch.

**1928:** On May 25 the Frank R. Howard Memorial Hospital was dedicated to the town of Willits, California, for community use by Charles and Fannie May Howard.

**1929:** Mr. Howard built a Children's Tuberculosis Hospital in the San Francisco Bay Area in California. In his final will he stipulated that in the event of this hospital's closure, all stocks and some materials were to be transferred to The Frank R. Howard Memorial Hospital in Willits, California. Mr. Howard died in 1950, and the Howard Childrens' Hospital closed in 1967. The proceeds from that Childrens' Hospital went to the start of the Frank R. Howard Foundation.

Also, from the Howard Childrens' Hospital, these items were moved to the Frank R. Howard Memorial Hospital in Willits, California:
(1) The pair of stone lion statues that recline on either side of the steps at the old front entrance of the Howard Hospital.
(2) The large oil painting of Frankie Howard and the dogs that is hanging in the halls.
(3) An elegant antique sideboard in the Hospital conference room where refreshments are served for their gatherings.

**1931:** Charles S. and Fannie May Howard's marriage was dissolved.

**1932:** Charles Howard, age 52, and Marcela Zabala, age 29, were married for what would be 18 years, until Mr. Howard's death. Marcela was the sister of Lin Howard Sr.'s wife, Anita.

**1933:** Seabiscuit was foaled at Claiborne Farm in Kentucky. He was not an impressive looking colt, and was kept in the background of that year's crop of foals.

Barbara B. Howard Collection

Frankie and Bob Howard with buck deer on old truck

Barbara B. Howard Collection

Frankie Howard ready for the Spring Roundup

**1934:** Charles and Marcela Howard were looking to expand their Throughbred racing stable.

**1935:** Charles Howard, Marcela and TrainerTom Smith increased their quest to improve their quality of horses, both at the racetrack and at Ridgewood Ranch.

**1936:** Fannie May married a San Francisco divorce laywer, William Herrscher.

**1936:** At the request of trainer Tom Smith, and with the approval of Marcela Howard, C. S. Howard purchased Seabiscuit, as a three year old, at the Saratoga Race Course in August for $8,000.

**1936-1940:** Seabiscuit's illustrious racing career thrilled the nation and the world. He became the World's Leading Money Winner, broke track records, won match races, and outran the best of the rest! (A very accurate portrayal of his racing years is found in Laura Hillenbrand's book *Seabiscuit: An American Legend.*)

**1939:** On April 10th of this year, Red Pollard married Agnes Conlon in St. Anthony's Catholic Church in Willits, California.

**1940:** Seabiscuit retired to stud at Ridgewood Ranch after winning the "Hundred Grander", (The Santa Anita Handicap) on March 2, 1940 on his third try. Seabiscuit ran second on his first two attempts in this race, the largest money race in the nation at that time. ( Handicap and foal records are in the back of this book *The Spirit of Seabiscuit* by Jani Buron)

**1940:** A book by B.K. Beckwith titled "Seabiscuit, The Saga of a Great Champion", claimed that Seabiscuit was awarded an Olympic medal for "Noteworthy Courage and Triumph". (The medal awarded has not yet been located or verified.)

**1941:** In December of this year, C. S. Howard purchased a large ranch eight miles west of Elko in Northern Nevada. Today this ranch is known as The Maggie Creek Ranch, and is still a very large operation. Mr. Howard's friend, Bing Crosby, also owned several ranches north of Elko. Mr. Howard kept his ranch until 1946.

**1941:** C. S. Howard collected a percentage on the sales of 30,000 new Buick motor cars!!

**1947:** May 17, 1947, Seabiscuit died suddenly of a heart attack at age 14. The Howard family and the whole Ranch, as well as the whole world, were in mourning. Seabiscuit sired 108 Thoroughbred foals while standing at stud.

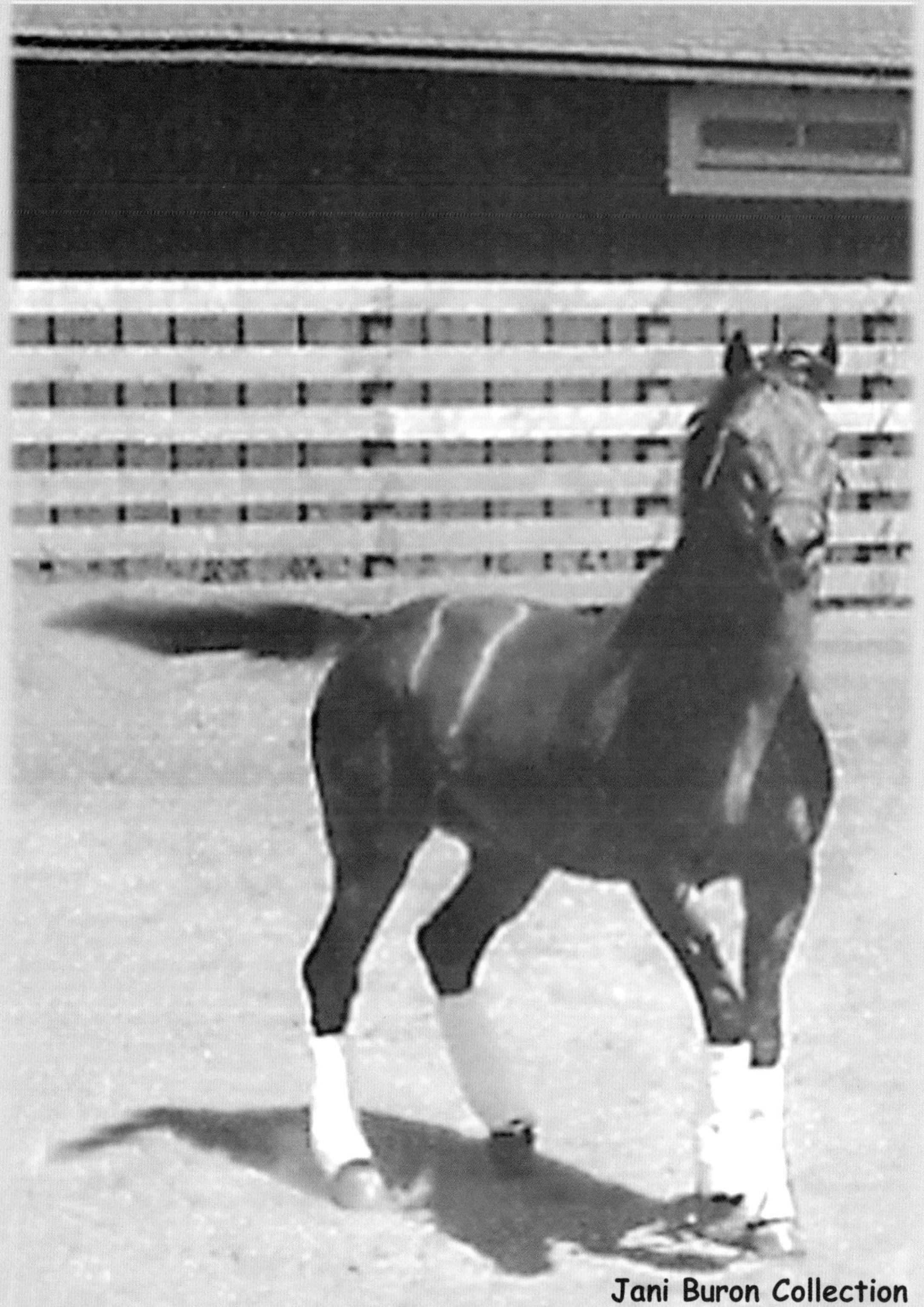

Jani Buron Collection

Seabiscuit first time free after the "Hundred Grander"

Above: A winter scene at the Maggie Creek Ranch

Below: Cattle on the ranch at the " Howard " time

Pictures courtesy of Northestern Nevada Museum in Elko, Nevada

**1950:** Mr. Howard's racehorse, Noor, won the Santa Anita Handicap. Noor also defeated the famous horse, Citation, four times and set new track records each time.

**1950:** Charles Stewart Howard, 73, died on June 6, 1950. The vast holdings of the Howard Estate were considered, and the family made decisions on what to sell and what to keep. After much thought, their decision was to sell some of the horses and other livestock at a dispersal sale, and to put Ridgewood Ranch on the market.

**1951:** The Welch Family of Oregon bought Ridgewood Ranch from the Howard Estate. They ran cattle and conducted a logging operation and built a mill in the meadow across Highway 101 from the familiar main Ridgewood Ranch entrance gate. Eventually the new Highway 101 Freeway was built higher up on the hill, above the Welch Brothers mill site and it bypassed the old entrance gate. To accommodate the new freeway, a new entrance to the Ranch was built further up on Ridgewood Grade. It remains there today. An old paved portion of Highway 101 crosses the new ranch entrance road, and goes on down into the Ranch at the original point of entry where the gate used to stand.

**1952:** Marcela Howard married Leslie Fenton, and they resided in Pebble Beach, California, where they built the Carmel Plaza shopping center. They also operated an antique shop there.

**1962:** Christ's Church of The Golden Rule purchased Ridgewood Ranch from the Welch Brothers. At the time of purchase, the working livestock part of the ranch remained much the same as it had when the Welches bought it from the Howard family.

**1976:** Mr. and Mrs. Leslie Fenton (formerly Marcela Howard) moved to Montecito, California, where Mr. Fenton passed away in 1978. They were married for 26 years.

**1987:** Marcela Zabala Howard Fenton passed away at age 84, one of her favorite memories to the end being the Seabiscuit years. She is remembered as a warm, delightful and compassionate lady.

**2001:** The book, *Seabiscuit; An American Legend,* written by Laura Hillenbrand, was released, and a movie was made of this wonderful Seabiscuit story of his racing years. This once again brought the exciting racing era of 1930-1940 alive for the American public, and drew attention to C. S. Howard's Ridgewood Ranch that was Seabiscuit's home in the 1940s.

**2002:** Mendocino County Museum in Willits, California opened a special Seabiscuit exhibit

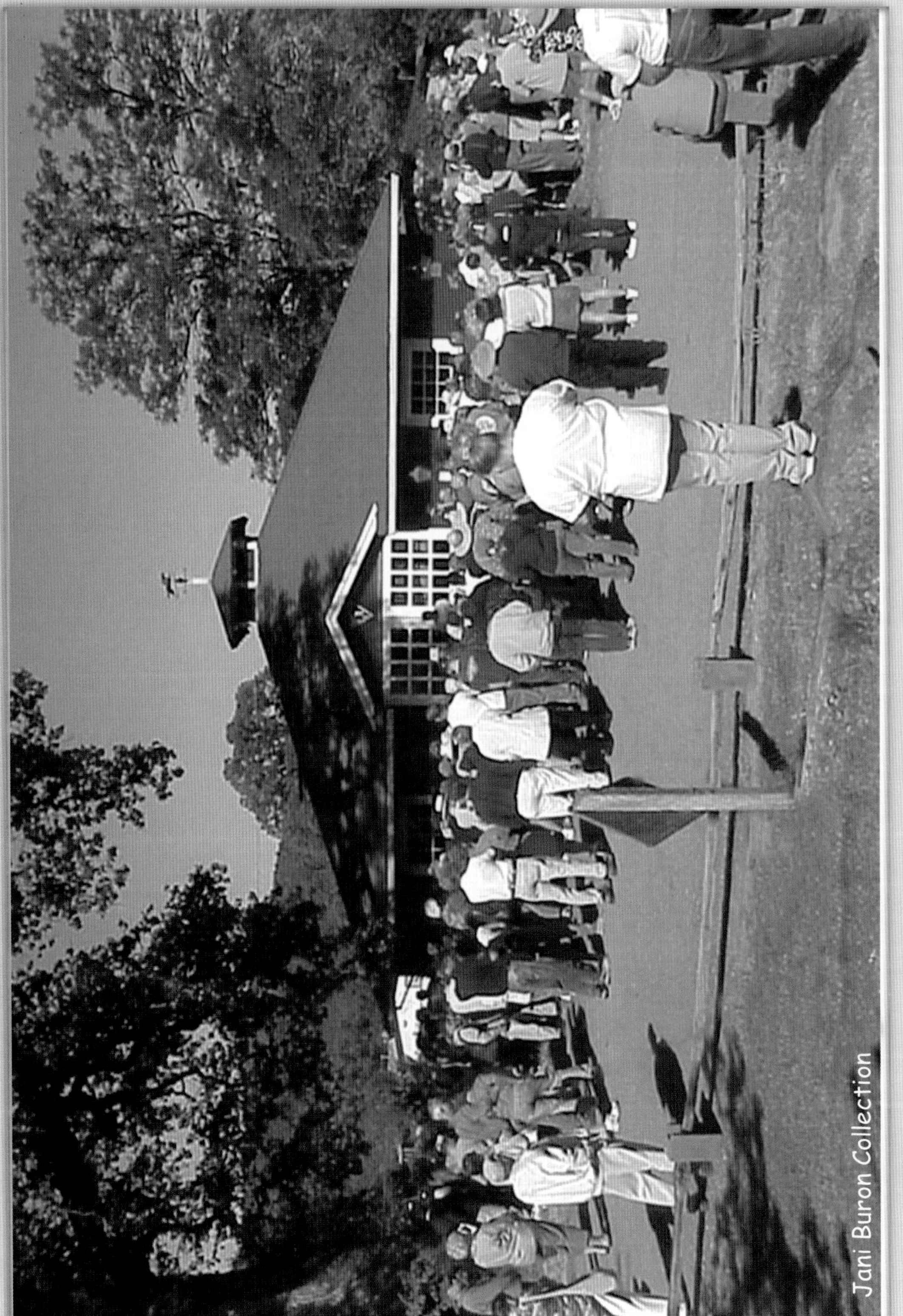

Jani Buron Collection

Ridgewood Ranch tour at dedication of restored Stud Barn, May 2004

filled with Seabiscuit memorabilia donated by individuals, and by Ridgewood Ranch. This exhibit is constantly being enlarged.

**2002:** The book, *Ridgewood Ranch, Home of Seabiscuit*, about Seabiscuit's retirement years, was written by author, Jani Buron, from her memoirs and was published in early May. She lived on Ridgewood in the 1940s and had many of her own photos of the ranch, and a vivid memory of ranch activities, of the Howards, and Seabiscuit.

**2002:** The first Ridgewood Ranch Walking Tour was offered on May 25 and quickly sold out, with an enthusiastic response from the public. More tours were added and it was clear that there was enough ongoing interest to plan for tours in 2003, also.

**2002:** The PBS Seabiscuit Documentary premiere showing was held at Ridgewood Ranch in November, as the 75th anniversary benefit for the Frank R. Howard Hospital. Mr. Howard built the hospital in memory of his son, Frankie, who received fatal injuries in an auto accident on the Ranch in 1926.

**2003:** The second season of Ridgewood Ranch Walking Tours was very popular, and the world premiere of the Universal movie *Seabiscuit* was shown at the Noyo Theater in Willits, California, on July 19, 2003. The event really put Willits on the map with the first benefit premiere in the country. The town was over-run with media people, newspaper and TV reporters, Seabiscuit fans and happy moviegoers. The movie was well done by the whole cast with standout performances from Jeff Bridges, Toby Maguire, Gary Stevens, Chris Cooper and Chris McCarron. PBS TV did a special on this event for their California Heartlands series titled *Seabiscuit*, program 749.**

**2003**: The A&E production of *The True Story of Seabiscuit* aired, and in December, ESPN II Classic SportCentury did a program on Seabiscuit. Each story is very well done and adds a little more to the legend.**

**2004:** May 29, on the first Ridgewood Ranch Guided Walking Tour of the third season, the restoration of the Stud Barn was dedicated and celebrated, with many of the Howard family members attending. Seabiscuit's barn is back! The tour season ended in October with full attendance and with as much enthusiasm as the first tour in 2002.

**The author, Jani Buron, appeared in these TV documentary productions along with others who are all a part of the Seabiscuit story.

Charles Stewart Howard

Fannie May Smith Howard

Center; Charles Stewart Howard

Left top: C. S. Howard Jr. Right top: Lindsay C. Howard Sr.

Left bottom: Frank R. Howard Right bottom: Robert S. Howard

## Howard Family Children

Charles Stewart Howard and Fannie May Howard had four children, all sons, and the family extends down through grandchildren, great-grandchildren and beyond, too numerous to mention them all here.

These are the four sons:

1. The first son, Charles Stewart Howard Jr, born in 1902, had two children:
   Charles Stewart Howard III, who had four children.
   Barbara Jean Howard Leask, who had two children.

2. The second son, Lindsay Coleman Howard, born in 1904, had six children:
   Mary (MyMy) Lynette Howard, who had two children.
   Lindsay Coleman Howard Jr., who had three children.
   Peter Stewart Howard, no children.
   Marcella Anne Howard, died at 4 days old.
   Frank Robert Howard, no children.
   Judith Linda Howard, who had two children

3. The third son, Frank (Frankie) Robert Howard,
   born in 1911, died at age 15 on Ridgewood Ranch.

4. The fourth son, Robert Stewart Howard, had two children.
   Robert Stewart Howard II, no children
   Leeann Howard, no children

<<<>>>

Charles Stewart Howard and his second wife, Marcela Howard, had no children.
Only Seabiscuit.

Barbara B. Howard Collection

Howards' Christmas 1925 at Ridgewood Ranch

Left to right: Dorothy and Charles S. Howard Jr., Frank R. Howard, Fannie May Howard.

Robert S. Howard, Charles S. Howard Sr., Lindsay C. Howard Sr. and wife, Anita.

## Frankie Howard

Charles and Fannie May Howard had their first two sons, Charles II and Lindsay, and then seven years later had Frankie and after that, Robert. The two older boys were married and on their own while the two younger ones were still at home.

Frankie loved animals, and he was a horseman, a hunter, a fisherman and a swimmer. Frankie always had a twinkle in his eye. Although he died as a young teenager, he did explore and enjoy life thoroughly while he was here. Friends and family helped him build a log cabin near a creek on Ridgewood Ranch. The cabin remained as it was, untouched, for many years after he died.

I don't know how many times Laverne, Betty and I rode by that cabin during the 1940's and looked at it sitting under the oak trees. We knew it sat dangerously close to a steep creek bank that washed under the cabin a little more each winter with high water. It is gone now.

We are reminded of Frankie because of the Frank R. Howard Memorial Hospital built in Willits, California, in 1928, by his father, as a tribute to the memory of his son. Mr. Howard wished to provide a suitable medical facility for the community that it had lacked before. Doc Babcock helped design and carry out the plan. Howard family members remained on the hospital board for years after it was completed. Mr. Howard had supplies from Ridgewood Ranch sent in daily, consisting of meat, vegetables, dairy products, and of course, flowers from the Ridgewood gardens.

The hospital today in 2006 is maintained by the Frank R. Howard Foundation and is privately run. The furtherment and improvement of the hospital facility is now underway with a new modern hospital planned to serve the Willits community and surrounding areas.

Barbara B. Howard Collection

Frankie Howard with his younger brother Robert S. Howard

Frank R. Howard being patriotic in an Uncle Sam outfit

## The Howard Brothers, Charles, Lindsay and Robert

C. S. Howard, who had been in the cavalry, was an excellent horseman, and naturally he wanted his sons to have the opportunity to become fine horsemen, too. He provided them with complete horsemanship training and the finest horses in the country. The two oldest boys, Charles II and Lindsay, became nationally recognized polo players and horse show participants. Lindsay's handsome horse named Ridgewood came from the ranch he was named for.

Lindsay later became involved in Thoroughbred racing, and was a partner with Bing Crosby in their Binglin Stables. The youngest Howard brother, Robert, also had racehorses, and after he passed on, his wife, Andrea, continued with the horses.

The familiar red and white Howard racing silks with the "Triangle H" are still seen on the racetrack today; the Howard family is still active and successful in racing some 70 years after C. S. Howard started his great racing stable. There are some fifth and sixth generation descendants of Seabiscuit still racing and winning today, in 2006.

Barbara B. Howard Collection

Lindsay C. Howard on his Polo Pony named "Ridgewood"

Marcela Zabala Howard

# MARCELA

Marcela Zabala Howard was an integral part of the Howard family. She was the sister of Anita Howard, Lindsay Howard Sr.'s wife, and therefore was acquainted with the Howard family early on. She was an actress, a fine horsewoman, and very well liked. She is remembered for her radiant smile, her generousity, her compassion, her love of horses and of Thoroughbred racing. She shared the same interest in fine horses as did Charles S. Howard Sr. They were wed in 1932.

Four years later, Charles and Marcela, at the urging of their trainer, Tom Smith, bought a three-year-old horse named Seabiscuit, who intrigued all of them. The Howards already had a winning racing stable, but Seabiscuit would be the one they were remembered for. During the depression years when people desperately needed something to lift their spirits, Seabiscuit provided hope as he became an American hero, American royalty, a household word and a horse revered for his determination, intelligence, heart, spirit, and winning ways. The little underdog horse from the West won against all odds time after time, and did so with class and finesse.

Marcela was a part of all this, and the wonderful Seabiscuit memories remained a part of her life for all of her days. After Charles Howard died in 1950, she remarried, but she remained close to Howard family members for the rest of her life. She is fondly referred to by the family as "Auntie Mar".

August 12 1938 Del Mar Racetrack, Seabiscuit beat Ligaroti in match race

## Seabiscuit - Ligaroti Story

This photo was taken at a very happy moment right after Seabiscuit won the much publicized match race against Ligaroti at Del Mar on August 12, 1938. Dixie Crosby is presenting the trophy to the winning owner, a smiling Charles S. Howard. On the left, Marcela Howard and Bing Crosby are looking on. To the right of his Dad, C. S. Howard, is Lin Howard. Lin and Bing were partners in the Binglin Stables and they owned Ligaroti. This race generated lots of excitement and speculation because of the rivalry between the two horses, the two owners, who were friends, and father and son from opposing racing stables. The grandstand had "cheering sections" set out that day, and due to wide publicity ahead of time, Del Mar had a standing room only crowd. That is what the main objective was, to draw attention to racing and to the then new California racetrack, Del Mar. It worked.

Jani Buron Collection

"Match Race of the Century". Seabiscuit winning the Pimlico Special

## Seabiscuit - War Admiral Story

The words "Match Race of The Century" immediately brings to the minds of horsemen everywhere, as well as Seabiscuit fans, the famous race between War Admiral and Seabiscuit. After much negotiating and "It's off" and "It's on" comments from the owners of both horses, the race was finally held at the Pimlico Racetrack in Baltimore, Maryland, on November 1, 1938. At one point, Samuel D. Riddle said he would not travel anywhere to run a match race against Seabiscuit. Charles S. Howard said he *would* ship from the West Coast to meet War Admiral at Pimlico.

The agreement between the two owners, Mr. Howard and Mr. Riddle, was a simple one page undated hand-typed document, probably done about the middle of September in 1938. A young Alfred Vanderbilt arranged to hold the race at Pimlico, where he was president at the time. Mr. Vanderbilt did a lot of negotiating to bring the race to a reality. Alfred approached Mr. Howard to sign the agreement at Belmont Park. Mr. Howard without hesitation signed it. Alfred waited at Pennsylvania Station in

New York City to see Samuel Riddle and get his signature on the agreement. Alfred got lucky, caught a reluctant Mr. Riddle at the station, got the signature and the race was on. The document reads as follows:

## PIMLICO MATCH RACE

BETWEEN WAR ADMIRAL AND SEABISCUIT TO BE RUN ON A FAST TRACK

DISTANCE: -One mile and three-sixteenths (3/16)

DATE: - First of November or third of November track must be fast decision by 8:30 to be made by Jarvis Spencer.

START: - Walk-up start, no stalls, from a flag. George Cassidy to start the race, no assistant starters to be on the track, a man suitable to both owners to use a recall flag in the event of a false start.

PURSE: - $15,000. to be added to the MARYLAND JOCKEY CLUB, all to the winner. In the event of a walkover, the MARYLAND JOCKEY CLUB to pay $5,000. to the horse walking over.

FORFEIT: - $5,000. Each owner to deposit a certified check for that amount with the MARYLAND JOCKEY CLUB to be held in the event of one horse not competing. [Added here in handwriting]: *in which event it goes to the horse walking over.*

CONDITIONS: - Each horse to carry 120 lbs.

Both horses to be examined by a veterinary both before and after the race.

I agree to the above conditions: - Charles S. Howard
Samuel D. Riddle
Alfred Vanderbilt

[Each affixed his own signature in ink, one below the other.]

Samuel Riddle had insisted on a walk-up start because War Admiral was often cantankerous and took aim at his handlers and the starting gate crew. Seabiscuit was spirited, but behaved well under most circumstances, and was also a great traveler, very relaxed. This rivalry situation of East Coast-West Coast provided the press with lots of material to write about. The two horses and their owners and everyone connected to them became the subjects of many a newspaper article. Speculation about who was the best horse was the talk of the day, and now it would soon be settled. People on the East Coast mostly favored War Admiral, the big black highly respected horse of Samuel Riddle's who had won the coveted Triple Crown. How could a little horse from the West Coast compete with a winner such as War Admiral! At age four, this race would be War Admiral's 23rd start and Seabiscuit's 84th start at age five. Plans were to retire War Admiral to stud the following spring. Seabiscuit would continue with his racing career as long as he was sound. He raced until 1940, when at age seven he was retired to stud as the world's leading money winner with $437,730. to his credit.

The day of the much anticipated big match race finally came. Seabiscuit fans crowded into the Pimlico grandstand early, and some fans went into the infield to watch from there. People who couldn't get into the stands stood and climbed to every available nearby perch to view the race. Citizens across America gathered by their radios to listen to it. Newspapers were poised to put out extra editions as soon as the race was run; even President Franklin D. Roosevelt put business at the White House on hold to listen to the greatest match race ever held. It was a great national event focused on two of the fastest horses that were racing at the time, competing for the title of being known as the best racehorse in America.

The two rival horses came out onto the racetrack for the post parade, #1 War Admiral with Charley Kurtsinger up and George Woolf doing the honors on the #2 horse, Seabiscuit, in place of a still recuperating Red Pollard. The crowd roared with excitement. No doubt a lot of patrons were trying to impress upon everyone around them why their favorite horse was the best and would win easily.

The onlookers watched breathlessly as the horses approached the point of the walk-up start. After two false starts, one attributed to each horse, the third start was the real go. War Admiral, who was on the inside, jumped up on his hind legs while Seabiscuit quickly scooted ahead and uncharacteristically took the lead, surprising many observers. By the time both horses reached the first turn, Seabiscuit was far enough ahead to be able to take position on the inside rail. Around the first turn and to the backstretch Seabiscuit had the lead. For several lengths down the backstretch, both horses ran as one, stride for stride. At one point George Woolf allowed War Admiral to get up very close to Seabiscuit. War Admiral took the lead by a head as Seabiscuit looked his rival in the eye, challenging him and showed his class by re-taking the lead.

As the horses reached the head of the homestretch, they were both trying hard to win. Seabiscuit clearly had something left, and War Admiral appeared to have given his all. Seabiscuit changed to his right lead coming into the stretch, and Woolf looked over at War Admiral and decided to go for it now. Woolf said to Charley Kurtsinger, "So long, Charley!" as he gave Seabiscuit a few taps of the whip. Biscuit responded, and drew out to a clear lead and won by four. Those three words Woolf coined created a classic new phrase heard often at the racetrack and across America. As Seabiscuit crossed the finish line a winner, the crowd went wild, the announcer is drowned out, and the celebration began all across America, especially on the West Coast. The little horse from the West has outrun the big Triple Crown Winner, the heavily favored blueblood horse from the East!

Barbara B. Howard Collection

Charles Sr., Andrea, Lin Sr. & wife Judith, Robert Sr. and Marcela, all Howards

The Howard team is ecstatic, the grandstand crowd is hysterical with joy, people are reaching out to touch Seabiscuit along the track rail and to grab any pieces of anything for a souvenir. The crowd control officers are over run and a happy pandemonium ensues. The press reporters begin to pound out stories on their typewriters of the gratest race ever run. As a proud Seabiscuit returns to the Winners Circle, he knows he has won. He is glad to see his friends, trainer Tom Smith and his owner Charles Howard there to greet him. An appreciative Mr. Howard shakes hands with a jubilant George Woolf, on Seabiscuit, while The Biscuit nibbles a special treat out of Tom Smith's hand. Someone thrusts a microphone into the winning jockey's face. George Woolf is extremely happy, and proud. George reflects on the confident feelings he had all along in his famous mount. He gives good credit to his buddy, jockey Red Pollard, who has just listened to the race from his hospital bed.

The media accounts of that unforgettable race, and in fact Seabiscuit's career, are good entertaining reading in themselves. The newspaper sports writers of that era wrote with originality and created great sport personality caricatures of the sports events of that day. Their description of the second by second action really gave an exciting picture of what went on. The radio sportscasters called it like it was, with great personal and descriptive enthusiasm and one got a good picture of every move in the race by just listening to the radio.

## A Traditional Gathering After An Occasion

Winning a race, big or small, traditionally was a call for celebrating to make a good thing better and to commemorate the occasion. Usually it was dinner and drinks with friends at a favorite restaurant. The day was rehashed and the races rerun and there was a general feeling of warmth and camaraderie. Perhaps that is the reason for the gathering pictured at the left.

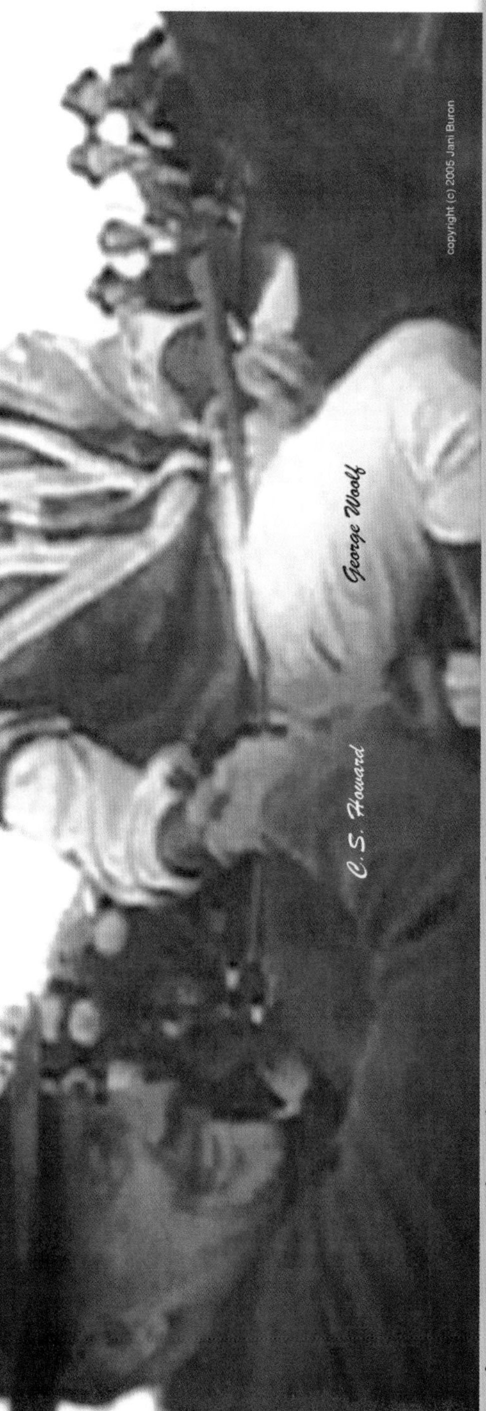


Charles Howard and George Woolf in the winners circle after beating War Admiral

# Chapter 1

## THE RIDGEWOOD BARN BUILDERS

Charles S. Howard got his start in business by being creative and by putting every bit of his income to good use toward a bigger and better way to make money. He had vision and foresight, and an appealing way of talking to other businessmen and getting his ideas across. By 1920 he became very successful with his Buick automobile dealerships on the west coast. He had worked hard to become financially independent, and now he could afford the time and the money to look around for his dream ranch. He found what he wanted in the Walker Valley, located in Mendocino County in Northern California. It was an ideal place to develop his dream of having a country place for his wife, Fannie May, and his four sons, Charles, Lindsay, Frankie, and Robert, to enjoy. It was also a favorable place for the self-sufficient, productive and working livestock ranch he had in mind.

When C. S. Howard first purchased Ridgewood Ranch, there was already a fine home on it that Mr. Van Arsdale had constructed. Mr. Howard designed and built an elaborate swimming pool and elegant bath house next to the home, and it was used and enjoyed by his family, his many friends, his ranch guests, as well as the children of the families who lived on Ridgewood. The home and the pool are still in use, and there for visitors to see today.

Mr. Howard then needed to customize the place and provide barns and corrals for the horses and cattle and other livestock he planned to have there. He would, of course, purchase the best materials available, and plenty of them. The triangle-wire fencing

The Howard pool by the family home at Ridgewood Ranch

Barbara B. Howard Collection
Frank R. Howard taking a dip in the new Howard pool at Ridgewood

The Upper Mare Barn when it was first built

Robert Lee Collection

(some call it "coyote-proof" wire) used for the fencing and cross fencing of the fields was designed so well and was made so stout that much of it still stands today. If you wanted it down, you had to take it down! The wire was strung up on big square sturdy Redwood fence posts, painted green, that came to a point on the top, which was painted white. The barns and the paddocks were built of the finest Redwood around. Some of them still stand today.

For several years most of the activity on the ranch involved regular ranching and livestock activities. Later, after Mr. Howard became interested in owning Thoroughbred race-horses, established himself at the racetrack, then purchased his great horse, Seabiscuit, that his idea for a Thoroughbred breeding farm came about. Spacious well built barns with large stalls to accommodate the foaling mares, with good paddock runs for their daytime use would be necessary, as well as a place for equipment needed in the barn at foaling time, and a place to stay for the watchmen on duty 24 hours a day.

In 1939 when Seabiscuit came home to Ridgewood to heal up from a racing injury, his regular jockey and friend, Red Pollard, was already there to greet him. Red was recuperating at Ridgewood from severe injuries to his right leg he had sustained in a bad fall from a horse at Suffolk Downs Racetrack. He was bedridden for months at Winthrop Hospital in Boston while the doctors efforts to heal his broken leg properly were unsuccessful. His nurse was Agnes Conlon, who later became his bride. Red's leg never did heal back to normal, so when he was released from the hospital, the Howards invited Red to come west and spend some time at Ridgewood. He had yet another accident while on the ranch and was put into the immediate care of Doc Babcock at Frank R. Howard Memorial Hospital. Doc re-broke and re-set the leg and this time it did heal up better, given enough care and rest. Seabiscuit healed up, too, along with Red, but very few people, other than the Howards and Tom Smith, thought either of them would ever be back on the racetack.

When Seabiscuit arrived at Ridgewood, he was stabled in an older barn near the Upper Mare Barn until his quarters in the new Stud Barn were ready. His bucket, feed tub, and medicine cabinet were hung on the barn wall outside his stall, racetrack style, and the tack box was set on the ground. All sported the "Triangle H" insignia and were painted in the Howard racing colors of crimson red and white. His stall door opened to the outside, where he could look out across the barnyard. He probably looked around for the racetrack, wondering when or where he would see it again. Meanwhile, he became interested in the comings and goings of life on Ridgewood where there were lots of new people, horses and other animals to get acquainted with.

Jani Buron Collection

The Lower Mare Barn in 1948, it was destroyed by fire in the 1950's

Meanwhile, Mr. Howard and Ec Safford selected the barn builders from the local community of Willits. The main contractor was Clarence Dart. Some of his crew members were George Pinches and his son, Sully Pinches, George Recagno and his brother, Pete Recagno, Lucky Johnson, and Neil Camp. Ec Safford was the Ridgewood Ranch manager at that time and his young son, Art, was learning to build and he helped on the barn crew.

Sully Pinches remembers that the Upper Mare Barn was built first, in 1939, when he was just out of school. He said the Redwood lumber was cut and milled in Eureka, California, then came by boat to the Union Lumber Company located in Fort Bragg, California. It was put on lumber trucks for the final haul from the Pacific Coast inland across the coastal hills of California to Ridgewood Ranch, south of Willits. Dana Fuller and Mr. Howard were good friends. The best quality paint that the Fuller Paint Company had to offer arrived at Ridgewood in 50 gallon drums. Lou Bassett hauled the gravel for the cement up from the nearby creek by horse-drawn wagon. It was a hard and heavy pull up the hill from the creek, so he changed to a fresh team of horses at noontime.

In the spring of 1940, the carpenter crew had completed their jobs of building the big new barns at Ridgewood; the Upper Mare Barn, the Lower Mare Barn, and the impressive new Stud Barn for Seabiscuit and the other Howard stallions to occupy.

Seabiscuit's retirement and homecoming to Ridgewood, after winning on his third try at the Santa Anita Handicap on March 2, 1940, was a glorious event. His victory in that final race had made him the leading money winner in the world with $437,730. to his credit. He was now seven years old. Mr. Howard had purchased him as a three year old for $8,000. His record reads 89 races, with 33 wins, 15 seconds, 13 thirds, plus 11 new track records at distances from five furlongs to a mile and a quarter, and he equaled two others. All of his accomplishments earned him a place in history as one of the greatest Thoroughbred champions of all time, and perhaps the most accomplished sports hero ever. Mr. Howard had notified the press and other dignitaries and many friends of the day of his famous horse's homecoming to Ridgewood.

When Seabiscuit was ready to unload, he walked down the ramp of his specially designed horse van. He was greeted by a sea of local citizens, reporters, movie cameras, and still cameras; ranch hands were there to attend to his every need. Seabiscuit posed royally for the cameras while looking around to check out the new surroundings.

Seabiscuit's homecoming was somewhat bittersweet, because he would not be racing again, something he truly loved; yet he was coming home to the beautiful

John Bosko Collection

Mr. Howard's favorite parade horse Chulo, he rode him often

Ridgewood Ranch in the Walker Valley, a very special place. Seabiscuit had left the racetrack for the last time, and would not see much of his racetrack friends Tom Smith, Red Pollard, or Pumpkin anymore.

Chulo, Mr. Howard's favorite saddle horse, came back to Ridgewood in the van with Seabiscuit. There were new acquaintances to meet upon arrival at the ranch, other animals, horses and new people. Now Seabiscuit could relax and eat and sleep all he wanted to. He would go on rides in the hills with Mr. Howard, and would learn a different way of life than he had experienced up to now. Then there was the business of reproducing Little Biscuits. Such a fine stallion with such great speed and heart must reproduce off-spring for the future of racing. Mr. Howard had purchased some well-bred Thoroughbred mares, planning to have a fine crop of "Little Biscuits" for the future. What Seabiscuit saw when he looked around to observe his new location was very inviting; large oak trees, green grassy hills, sparkling creeks, blue skies, tall pine trees, big barns with spacious stalls, large pastures and paddocks; and best of all, the Howards were there!

The Stud Barn was designed and built to accommodate four stallions, the feed room where custom grain feeds were mixed for them, and the ground floor quarters for the man in charge of the Stud Barn who lived there and was on duty 24 hours a day. He also acted as the tour guide for the many visitors who came to see Seabiscuit. The barn had a pair of wooden sliding doors on either end, with little square-pane windows in the top part of each door. Wood flooring was at each entrance, with red cork-brick floor in the center of the barn between the corners of the four stalls. The bricks gently sloped down to a brass water drain in the middle. The horses were bathed over this area, and then they were brushed and groomed until they shined. Seabiscuit enjoyed his grooming routine because he knew he would then be turned out in his paddock where he could go roll in the soft dirt.

Four Howard studs including Seabiscuit occupied the finished four-stall Stud Barn. Seabiscuit in 1940, Kayak II in 1941, with Mioland, Sabu and Ajax arriving later. Another stud on the ranch, Son Of Battle, who was kept at a different barn, had inherited some of the aggressive dominating characteristics of his background stock. He had the disposition of an angry lion. When he got out one time, he went directly for Mr. Howard's favorite parade and saddle horse, Chulo. He got in with Chulo and savaged him, fighting for dominance. Chulo was badly injured, and so Mr. Howard had the barn building crew quickly build a large-animal operating table with a convertible top. The top could be tipped up to a vertical position, and the horse placed next to it mildly sedated, strapped to the table, then fully sedated, and the table could be tipped back to a horizontal

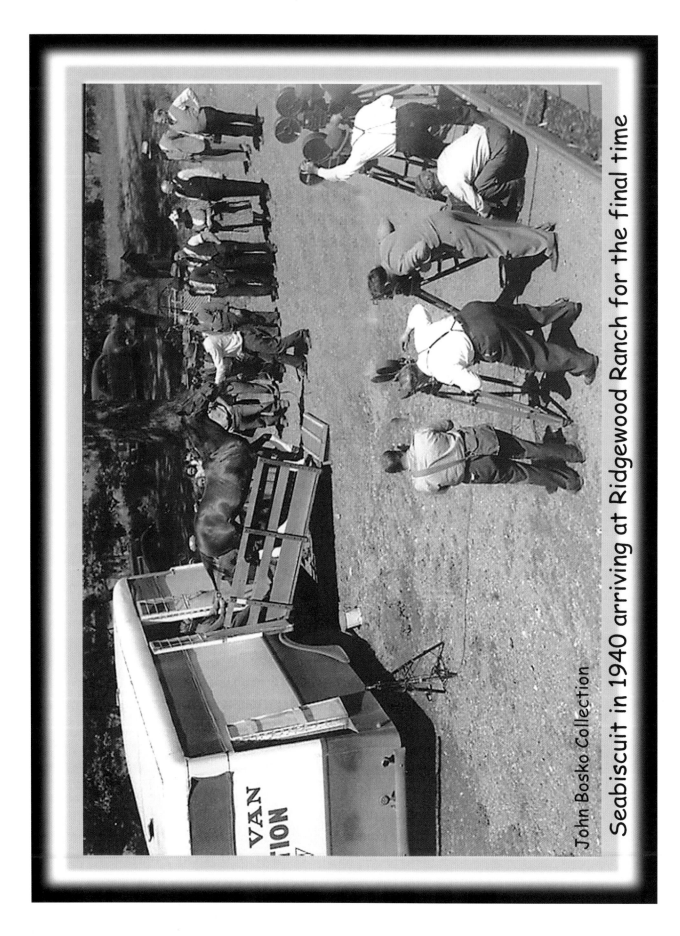

John Bosko Collection

Seabiscuit in 1940 arriving at Ridgewood Ranch for the final time

John Bosko Collection

Seabiscuit getting acquainted at Ridgewood Ranch. Ec Safford at right

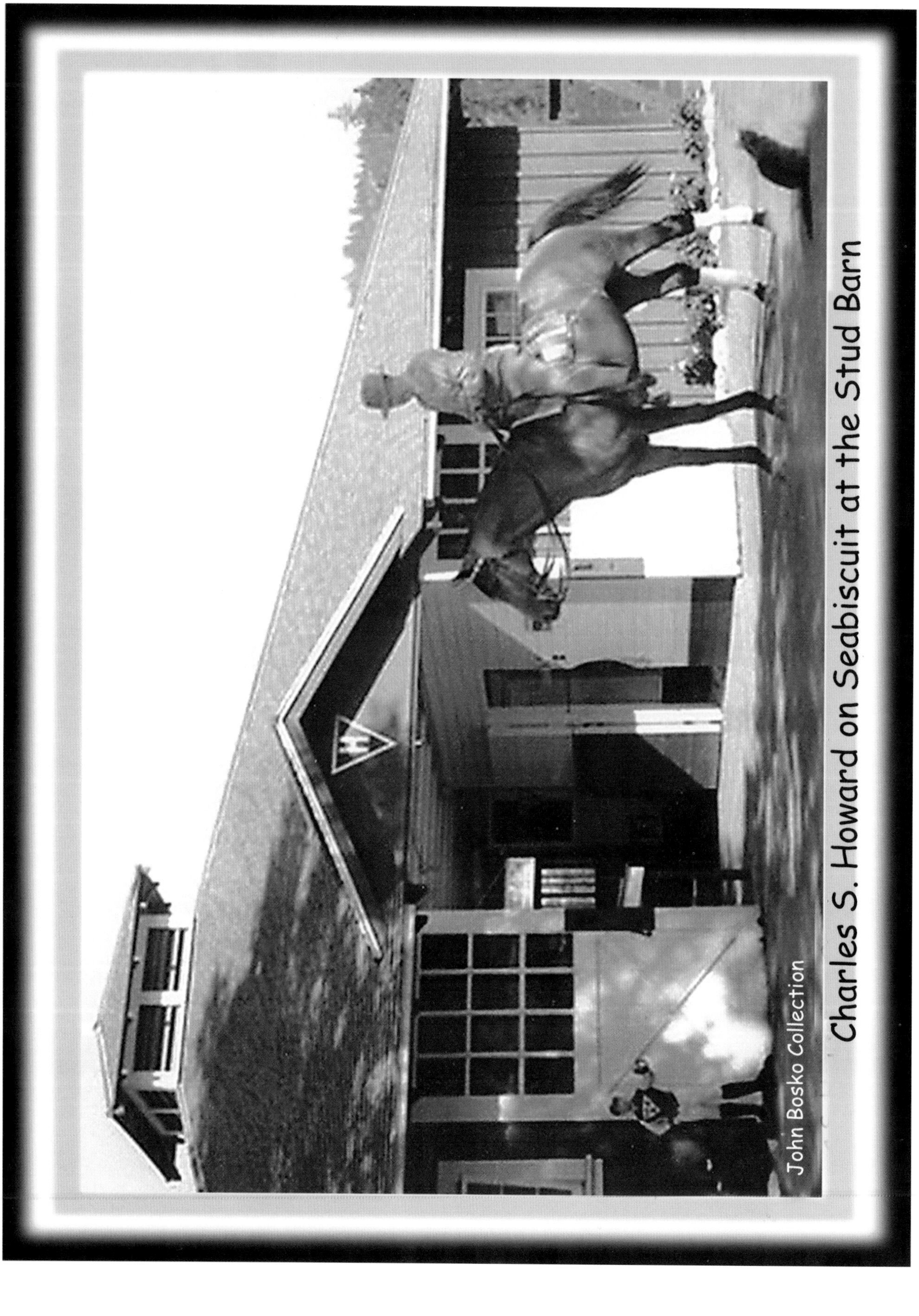

Charles S. Howard on Seabiscuit at the Stud Barn

John Bosko Collection

position so the attending doctor could work on him. Doc Babcock from Willits was called upon to stitch up the many injuries to Chulo's hide. Sully said it took Doc a whole day to sew up Chulo. The horse recovered quite nicely, and the scars were not highly visible. Mr. Howard and Doc were very good friends. Mr. Howard was appreciative of Doc's diversified medical talents, and he gave Doc a new Buick automobile each Christmas.

After the three barns were built at Ridgewood, the Upper Mare Barn, The Lower Mare Barn, and the Stud Barn, some of the building crew, including George and Sully Pinches, continued to build for Charles Howard at his San Ysidro ranch in Southern California. They built the biggest barn of all down there. They had a training track at San Ysidro for the young horses who were brought down from Ridgewood, among them the Seabiscuit yearlings. A hay crop grew in the training track infield, and with the good growing climate in that part of the country, the hay crop grew quickly, and was mowed once a month. The young horses also spent some of their training time at the Caliente Racetrack in Tijuana that was just across the California-Mexican border from the Howard Ranch at San Ysidro.

Sully Pinches recalls being at San Ysidro on Pearl Harbor Day, Sunday, December 7, 1941, when World War II began with the Japanese surprise attack on Pearl Harbor. With so many of America's young men called upon to defend their country, the young men of the summer hay crews at Ridgewood were gone off to war, so the older men then came to help put up the hay, among them Lou Bassett, with his teams and wagon.

World War II changed the lives of the whole American population. The young women went to work in the defense factories, and the older women once again became teachers, store workers and telephone operators. They also took turns watching for approaching enemy planes in the Western sky from the lookout towers on the high peaks such as Iron Mountain and Signal Mountain near Laytonville. Enemy war planes were expected to attack the port cities of San Francisco, Seattle and Los Angeles, and their choice of entry pattern could be anywhere along the Pacific Coast. When the town siren signaled a "blackout drill", we all took safety measures. We never knew at the time if the siren was only a drill, or for real. If the siren sounded at night, we immediately lowered the black roller shades that were in place on every window, and turned off all lights except for one low light, or a candle, in the middle of the room away from the windows. Sometimes we used only flashlights to light our way around the house. This made the houses and towns almost invisible from the air, in case an enemy war plane was overhead. A blast of the "all clear" siren would signal that the danger had passed.

Northeastern Nevada Museum Collection

This barn at the *Maggie Creek* Ranch was built in mid 1800's and is still in use today

Shortages of supplies and materials at home that were being used for the war effort brought about the ration book system. Each family was periodically issued a book of ration stamps that limited their purchase of certain grocery items, shoes, gas, and whatever other items may contain materials used for the war effort. The needs of the military came first, and no amount of money could buy more goods than your ration book allowed. This brought about some creative trading among the townfolk for certain items needed more by one family than by another. Everyone was united behind the country's defense and the cause for winning the war. The automobile gas shortage during wartime was one reason that not many outside mares were brought the long distance to Seabiscuit's court.

In 1940 the barn building crew built the main Ridgewood entrance gate that was so familiar to the travelers on Highway 101. It was made of four tall Redwood logs upright, two on the right, two on the left, and one log across the top. George Recagno recalls that while they were in the building process, they put up a temporary 2"x4" board across the top to span the upright logs. Someone dared George to walk across that board ... and he did it! While he was up there, he then realized just how far off the ground it was! Mr. Howard put up a red and white sign on top of it proclaiming that this place was, indeed, "Ridgewood Ranch, Home of Seabiscuit"! He was so very proud of his great champion horse.

George left his job at Ridgewood when he was drafted to serve in the Army Air Force for World War II in March of 1941. He served for five years, and became a pilot of P-51's, flying 132 missions.

George has a very special item in his home that at one time belonged to C. S. Howard. It is a large wooden dining room table made of beautifully grained walnut, with a lovely ornate design carved onto the edge trim. It has leaves to stretch it out so the eleven chairs that came with it, including a Captain's Chair, can be seated. The history of the table, and how it came to be in George's home is interesting.

To begin with, C. S. Howard donated the table to the City of Willits for use in their offices. George was on the Planning Commission for 18 years, and he sat at that table for their meetings. Eventually, as the city offices changed and grew, then moved, to another location, the table became the property of the Fire Department. When it was no longer needed there, it came up for sale. George bought the treasure, and put it to use in his house where it is still in use today, with George still sitting at that same table!

To. Jack Robbins.
Who loves 'Biscuit as much as we do.
Charlie & Marcela Howard – 10/12/42

Maggie Creek Ranch Collection

Seabiscuit exercising at Santa Anita racetrack with jockey George Woolf in the irons. This picture is on display at the Maggie Creek Ranch office in Elko, Nevada.

## THE ELKO CONNECTION

During the early 1940's C.S. Howard and Marcela decided to buy another ranch. He was an astute businessman. If he was interested in something, he looked into it, investigated it, got to know it, and then if he liked it and it suited his business procedures, he bought it. He had his Buick automobile agencies, his home in the San Francisco Bay Area, a Childrens' Tuberculosis Hospital, The Frank R. Howard Memorial Hospital in Willits, California, his successful Thoroughbred racing stables, Ridgewood Ranch as Seabiscuit's home, a training ranch at San Ysidro, as well as many other interests.

At some point in time, Mr. Howard became interested in property near Elko, Nevada. His friend, the crooner Bing Crosby, owned some large ranches north of Elko, as well as some other properties in the area. Bing and his family became a part of the Elko community.

In 1941, Charles and Marcela Howard bought property about eight miles west of Elko (near the Hunter railroad siding) that is now called Maggie Creek Ranch. It was called The Howard Ranch, a 2500 head cow operation, a large spread of 47,000 acres then, that is considerably larger now. His cattle were branded with the famous "Double H" iron. The "Double H" brand was an HH , joined together in the middle, and it was first registered in 1873 in Nevada by the Hunter family, who had previously owned the ranch. The Howards had this ranch until 1946 when he sold it to the Strathearn Cattle Company of Simi, California. C. S. Howard was well known to the local community of Elko. Even though he could not spend much time there because of his other businesses, they were aware that he was the owner of the great racehorse, Seabiscuit, and he had many friends in Elko.

Bing Crosby was elected to the position of Honorary Mayor of Elko. Bing and Mr. Howard had a mutual interest in fine race horses, and their famed match race that Seabiscuit won against Ligaroti at the Del Mar Racetrack in California was still talked about. Both men also liked Elko and owned ranches there. Bing often visited Mr. Howard at his Ridgewood Ranch in Willits, California, during the 1940's.

Bing Crosby brought some friends of his who were Hollywood stars up to Elko for the world premiere movie showing of "Here Comes The Groom" in July of 1951 at the Hunter Theater, among them Alexis Smith and Dorothy Lamour. The proceeds of the showing benefited the Elko Hospital Fund.

The well-known photograph of Seabiscuit galloping around the racetrack with George Woolf up is framed and hanging on the wall of the office of the ranch foreman, Jon Griggs, at the Maggie Creek Ranch today. On the front it is inscribed:

*"To Jack Robbins - who loves 'Biscuit as much as we do. Charlie and Marcela Howard, 10/12/42"*

On the back of the picture is this handwritten note:

*"Howards owned a lot of Hunter-Banks Ranch at one time. C. Evans thought someone at Maggie Creek should have this."*

On an aged yellow post-it note beside those words, is this message:

*"Walt L. gave this to Wayne M. to take to ranch - if they want it."*

They did want it; the photo hangs in a place of honor as a reminder of the C. S. Howard-Elko connection. Jack Robbins, the first name on the photo, was an Elko attorney and a good friend of Mr. Howard. "Wayne M." refers to Wayne Martini, who was the foreman of the Maggie Creek Ranch for many years. His wife, Della, still lives there on the ranch. The reference to the "Hunter-Banks Ranch" is what that property was known as since the early 1870's, and is still referred to by that same name sometimes today, even though that piece of land has been through several other ownerships.

A handsome gentleman living in Elko named Eddie Murphy, who was born in Cherry Creek, Nevada, over 103 years ago, recalls Mr. Howard owning the ranch in Elko, but what Eddie remembers more is that he traveled all the way to Oakland, California, to purchase a Buick automobile from the Howard Automobile Agency. The new Buick was a green coupe with a rumble seat! He did this in the wintertime, and the snow prevented any road travel over the Sierra Nevada Mountains, so Eddie and his new car traveled back to Reno, Nevada, on the train that went through the snow sheds along the mountain route. From Reno, he drove the new Buick back to his Cherry Creek ranch. In 1958 Eddie and his family moved to Elko, Nevada, where he eventually served in the Nevada State Assembly (Rep) for three terms in 1919, 1923, and 1929. His son, E. C. Murphy Jr., served in the same position for the two terms of 1959 and 1961.

# Chapter 2

## THE FIRST TIME AT RIDGEWOOD

In 1940, my Dad, Chet Griffith, worked at Seabiscuit's new home, Ridgewood Ranch. The owner of Ridgewood Ranch C.S. Howard and Dad became good friends right away, and they enjoyed working together. They were introduced to each other earlier by Dink Persico, a mutual friend of theirs from Willits. The first time that my Dad worked on Ridgewood we lived in a small community north of Willits called Laytonville, in a little house called "Day's House" on the main street, which was also Highway 101.

My Mom taught grade school there, and High School music and art. Dad stayed at Ridgewood Ranch during the week, and we would go visit him there on weekends. Sometimes he would come home to Laytonville on his days off. On those early visits to Ridgewood, even though I was very young, I truly enjoyed getting acquainted with the horses and the other animals. I looked forward to those times at that great big ranch, and felt that valley was very special. There was always something new to see, and good things happened there. I met a horse named Seabiscuit who lived there.

Looking back at all the times I went by Seabiscuit's paddock and saw him napping under the oak tree, or saw Mr. Howard riding his prize stallion around the ranch, or watched Seabiscuit's foals developing, I know now that we just took all that for granted, and it was really all so special. Seabiscuit truly is one of the immortals in Thoroughbred racing history.

While we lived in Laytonville, World War II was in full swing. My Grandma was a "lookout lady", and took shifts watching the sky for enemy war planes. I remember seeing the Army troops coming through town in slow-rolling caravans of camouflage vehicles. The open trucks held troops standing up in the back, and we stood at attention and saluted them and waved our small hand-held American flags to them as they passed through. The news of them coming spread far ahead of their arrival, and the town women baked and prepared goodies as fast as they could, handing their packages up to the soldiers in the truck as they went slowly by. I saw lots of happy smiles of appreciation on those faces of our men in uniform who were going off to war.

While we were cheering our troops as they passed through Laytonville, the same thing was happening further on down Highway 101 in Willits. A young girl named Annette Deghi moved to Willits with her family during the days of World War II. She remembers the troop trains that stopped at the railroad station near "John's Place", which was her parents' place of business on Commercial Street. The family living quarters were upstairs over the business, and because Annette was so little, her Mom told her to stay upstairs most of the time. But when the soldiers came through on the trains and were allowed to go to John's Place for a rest stop and refreshments, Annette had a job to do. She came downstairs and sat on a chair by the jukebox and handed out large photos of Seabiscuit to the soldiers. The soldiers really liked having a photo of the champion horse signed by Mr. Howard himself. They liked receiving them from a pretty little girl like some of the daughters they left behind when they went in the Army. Mr. Howard made sure they always had a good supply of photos on hand, and Annette remembers going down to Ridgewood Ranch with her family to pick them up.

When a blackout siren sounded in Willits, and the dark shades were pulled over the windows of all the establishments, Annette's family would go downstairs until the all clear siren sounded. Annette's Mom instructed her to stay safely under the large table, and her Mom would teach her to count to 100 to take her mind off being scared. Annette had an older brother who went into the service, and someone once told them that they heard on the radio that his ship, The U.S.S. Calhoun, had been hit by a Kama-Kazi plane and had blown up. At first they did not believe it, but later came to know that it was true, but that her brother had survived the attack OK.

Annette's family attended St. Anthony's Catholic Church in Willits, which is where Charles and Marcela Howard went when they were staying at their Ridgewood home. The Howards' helped the church out in many ways. Marcela once brought in a lovely set of six cups with a horse design on them to be raffled off, and Annette won them. Annette still displays those cups in her home today.

St. Anthony's Church is where Seabiscuit's jockey, Red Pollard, married his bride, Agnes Conlon, on April 10, 1939. They fell in love while she was his attending nurse in the Winthrop Hospital in Boston, Massachussetts. Red had received serious injuries in a fall, and his crushed leg would not heal, so he spent several months in the hospital. He eventually came to California to the Frank R. Howard Memorial Hospital in Willits, where Doc Babcock was successful in getting Red's leg to heal properly. Red stayed at Ridgewood later while both he and Seabiscuit healed up together.

At some time while Dad was working at Ridgewood in the early 1940's, Mr. Stempel made him a more tempting offer to come to work at his Willowbrook Ranch in Sherwood Valley that was closer to where we lived in Laytonville. Mr. Stempel and Mr. Howard were friends, and both were San Francisco businessmen. Mr. George Stempel was known as "The Donut King" for his pastry shop, Stempel's Donuts, located in downtown San Francisco. Charles Howard owned the large Buick agency on Van Ness Avenue in San Francisco. They both owned race horses. Just like with their race horses, there was a competitiveness in their friendship. They both liked my Dad's way of working with the horses, so they both made him offers to work on their ranches.

Mr. Stempel had some Thoroughbred stallions and mares at Willowbrook, and he had an interest in racing. Mr. Howard was known for owning the world champion Seabiscuit and Ridgewood Ranch. We heard that one Christmas, Mr. Stempel designed a Christmas card to send to C. S. Howard that showed a picture of his average stud, Put In, beating Howard's immortal Seabiscuit at the finish line! They both had a good laugh over that!

Dad did decide to go to work as the ranch foreman on Stempel's Willowbrook Ranch, which was nice because it was closer to Laytonville, and he could come home more often. We continued to live in Laytonville until Mom finished out the school year, and when a house became available on Willowbrook, we moved up there. We also knew by the time we moved that we would have a new little brother or sister sometime in October of 1944!

Willowbrook Ranch was located north of Willits up off the old stagecoach road that leaves Highway 101 just north of town.The road travels through Sherwood Valley past the various ranches, the school, and then returns to Highway 101 at a point several miles north of Willits and a few miles south of Laytonville. This road to Sherwood was at one time the main north-south route in this part of the country. When Highway 101 was built, it bypassed Sherwood Valley. Highway 101 became known as The Redwood Highway, and was very popular with travelers and tourists. The little town of Sherwood became deserted as folks moved out to be nearer to the centers of commerce along the new highway. The railroad was soon abandoned and Sherwood Valley became very quiet, populated by only the ranching families.

Sherwood was definitely a ghost town by the time we lived there. Someone was living in the old post office, for lack of any other suitable quarters. The Sherwood Hotel was still standing, but neglected. All of the doors and windows were missing due to the ravages of time. Once it had been a very inviting hotel, and now the range cows roamed freely in and out of the building. The building still stood straight and true, and the handsome structural lines of the exterior remained intact. That building always intrigued me, for what reason I did not know. I just enjoyed looking at it and could imagine how it was in its heyday with people coming and going in the once lively town of Sherwood. The building has since been restored and is now a ranch home, suitably occupied by an old Sherwood family.

We went to help the James family with their Spring roundups that were held in the corrals just below the old hotel across Sherwood Road. The James Ranch corrals were at the edge of a large meadow where the town was once located. The raised train track bed was still visible, and remnants of building foundations still marked the site. This place had once been full of activity as the business owners and people of the old town of Sherwood went about their daily activities.

The food tables for the noonday meal at the roundup were set up next to the old hotel building in the lacy shade of the blossoming apple trees. The sweet smelling blossoms of these ancient apple trees filled the air. What a wonderful playday for kids! The open hotel building, the orchard above the road, the corrals below where the marking and branding action was taking place and the surrounding hillsides full of Spring wildflowers! Lots of excitement, lots of wonderful food, and the whole day to play with the kids from the neighboring ranches!

The Sherwood Valley ranches were too far apart for us children to see much of each other or to go on rides together. I was about seven at the time, and already riding by myself. Dad had me on a horse before I could walk, so I do not remember learning how to ride; I just always knew how. I recall Dad giving me specific pointers about riding and taking care of horses. He was very serious about good horsemanship and the proper care and feeding of livestock. He worked on different ranches when I was very young, and we were always around horses, cattle and all other ranch animals.

There were two horses I could ride anytime, just around the Ranch; a sweet old brown mare, Babe, and a brown and white gelding named King. Babe was slow, easy riding and very dependable. Babe was kind of swaybacked, and had a round belly anyway, so no one noticed when she was getting rounder. She surprised everyone that year by producing a beautiful little colt! Babe had to take care of her baby now, so that is when I rode King a lot more. King went a little faster, and was a better seat as a bareback ride.

I rode King around the part of the ranch we lived on, and then on over the hill to the other part of the ranch where the big barn and little training racetrack were. The cookhouse was also here, the tractor shed, the chickens, and pigs, milk cows, the saddle horses and work horses. When I rode over the hill directly in back of our house, along the fenceline trail, I went past our favorite swimming hole. It was a place where the river slowed down and flattened out, forming a large shallow area where kids could play safely, as well as a deep part next to the rocks where the swimming was good. It was really a good place to skip flat rocks across the water; you could skip them all the way to the other side of the river. There was a good supply of small flat stones all over that part of the riverbed. There was also a neat path of large stepping stones from one side of the river to the other.

Once over that hill, past the river, the trail came down into the sawmill that was on the ranch. The people that operated that mill were members of Christ's Church of The Golden Rule, and they came from somewhere in the Central Valley. Their children attended the Sherwood school with me. When I went to visit them at their little mill cabins, we sometimes went down to the company store that was on the property to get supplies for their Mom, and a little treat for us too. They were there for only part of the year, as the mill operation was seasonal. The same families returned each year, so we got to know each other and be good friends. When the mill kids were not there, the school attendance went down to anywhere from one to five students. The entire sawmill operation was located there in that meadow at the edge of the woods; the huge saw table shed, the tall ever-burning boiler stack, and the decks of logs. The cabins and the company store were on the hillside next to it. If I rode on past the mill, we came to the main part of Willowbrook where most of the ranching activity was.

In October of 1944, when I was seven, and we were living at George Stempel's Willowbrook Ranch in Sherwood, it was getting close to time for Mom to have my baby brother. She had three false labors, and we rushed her into Willits each time, and the last time, Doc Babcock said, "No more going back to the ranch for you, it is too far out and you may not get here in time , and you need to deliver that big baby here in the hospital!" So Mom and I moved into Willits, and Grandma came up to stay with us, too, to take care of Mom. We stayed at the Pepperwood Motel on Main Street.

From The Pepperwood Motel, I remember going down to Quadrio's Store, dragging my "wagon" made of a cardboard box with a pull rope, and taking my Raggedy Ann and Andy dolls for a ride. I would get what Mom needed in the way of a few groceries, and a soda or an ice cream for me. One of the Quadrio brothers "played magic" and would pretend to "pull" quarters and dimes he saw sticking out of my ears or my nose! "See, this was in your ear! It is yours, and you can buy something with it!" That store had everything in it from long salamis hanging overhead to great wheels of cheese sitting on the counter, to shoes, school clothes, work clothes, and everyday dresses and dress-up attire for women. The sign painted onto the store front read: "Quadrio Brothers Gen. Merchandise and Groceries".

After about two weeks of living in town, my brother, John, was born at the Howard Hospital in Willits. He was delivered by Doc Babcock at high noon on October 18, 1944. Dad came in to town to see his new son, and then he took me back home, and Grandma went back home to Hopland where she taught school.

While my Mom and baby brother were resting up in the hospital, Dad and I were home at the ranch. During that time, a huge forest fire got started in the Sherwood Valley. It quickly became very fast moving, unpredictable, and dangerous. We never knew where the fire was going to jump to next. Dad kept me with him every minute for safekeeping, and he never let me out of his sight. In the daytime I rode around with him in the ranch pickup. I remember seeing my first bear then, while sitting in the pickup waiting for Dad. The frightened bear was running out of the burning woods seeking safety across the meadow just below our house. The fire raged on for a few more days, until the weary firefighters and ranchers finally got the upper hand. When it was safely out, we brought Mom and my new baby brother home after a two-week stay in the hospital. Mom was really glad to get home.

The Jones family came to visit us while we were at Willowbrook. Their two girls, Laverne and Betty, were my age. Curley Jones and my Dad had met the first time Dad worked at Ridgewood. Curley still worked at Ridgewood. Since the girls were ranch kids, too, we became friends right away. My Mom gave Laverne and Betty music lessons later, so we got to visit often.

We lived on at Willowbrook a while longer. While we were there, an opportunity came up to buy a modern new truck with a fifth-wheel six horse van with a small living quarters in the back. After much thought Dad bought it, and used it to haul a few horses around locally, and found that it was really a well built vehicle, being low-to-the-ground, and went down the road very smoothly. It gave the horses a good comfortable ride, and they shipped well in it. Dad decided that one day he might try making his living at hauling horses on the racetrack, which there was a demand for at the time. The future of Willowbrook seemed uncertain right then, too.

After one of his first horse hauling trips, Dad drove the van home from Willits up the Sherwood Road to Willowbrook one time ... and one time only; the reason being a sharp left-angle turn at the end of a bridge that the long fifth-wheel van could not negotiate. He eased partway around the turn at the end of the bridge and then suddenly the van's back left set of wheels slipped into midair over the steep creek bank. The van was suspended there, the back left corner sagging down toward the creek. Dad couldn't drive forward, and he certainly couldn't back up. Dad had thought about turning the van around earlier to go back, but the road had been too narrow at any point on the road before this bridge. So he had to try to negotiate this sharp turn; there was no other choice.

It was daylight when the horse van became stranded on the bridge. People came from nearby ranches to help out right away, but it was well into the night before all the helpers that came to the strange scene figured out how to get the van around the turn and off the bridge. The road was completely blocked all this time.

The news traveled fast around Sherwood about the big horse van blocking the bridge. This was done by means of the "country grapevine", otherwise known as the party line telephone! The party line system was the farmers phone line that went to each house along the road. When one party rang up a party at another house, those rings were heard at every house along the way. Each household had their own ring, like "two long, one short", or "one long, one short", "two long"; sometimes the distinction between "long" and "short" was not always easy to discern, depending upon just how the person cranking the ringer spaced the turns on the crank. There was also an "emergency ring" in each community that called everyone to the phone for an emergency announcement of some kind, like if someone needed help quickly. With all these different rings, people would often pick up the phone to see if the call was for them. Then the conversations started. Any conversation on this party line could quickly become general knowledge, intentional or not. So this is how the news of the horse van stuck on the bridge rapidly spread through the Sherwood community.

With the gathering crowd, someone finally brought some long strong enough planks that were placed under the wheels to span the space between the bridge and the bank. The planks rested securely on solid ground at both ends. The back tires on the van could then get traction, get level and roll on over the planks. There was a lot of backing and turning, inch by inch during this process, with a lot of people calling out directions from all sides of the stranded horse van. Finally Dad was able to get the van eased back onto the road. Neighbors had brought food and coffee to sustain the working crew, which was a long standing automatic custom with country folk. Dad got out, he thanked everybody for coming to help and had a cup of hot coffee. I think there was a little bottle of spirits being passed around that night to sweeten the coffee. He then got back into his van and continued on his way to Willowbrook as a collective sigh of relief went up from the crowd of helpers. On the return trip, the road allowed enough room on the other side to get the

Robert Lee Collection

The first one room school in Sherwood Valley, for grades 1 through 8

van slowly around the same sharp turn and across the bridge without any mishaps. After that scary experience, when the van wasn't in use, Dad parked it somewhere in Willits, or in the large flat barnyard down at Ridgewood Ranch, instead of trying to drive it up to Willowbrook.

While Dad worked at Willowbrook, he owned a Thoroughbred racehorse named Willow Count that he hired someone to train and race in Northern California. Dad planned to eventually be at the racetrack and train his own horses later. He brought Willow Count home to Willowbrook Ranch from the racetrack to rest up one time and what a contrast that horse was to the ranch saddle horses I had been around! He was tall and rangey, and high strung. Dad kept reminding me to not walk around behind him, or too close to the front of him! This long legged chestnut horse seemed to tower over me, and there was sure nothing laid-back about him. He was always on the muscle, moving around.

Later on, Dad decided to leave Willowbrook and go full-time into the horse hauling business. At that time, Mom was the only teacher available to teach at the one-room Sherwood school, where she was teaching all eight grades. The students were made up of us ranch kids and a few mill kids, and that only totaled about a dozen or so at the most, on a good day. The number of students in attendance went up and down through the year, and at times, I was the only student in that school! They kept it open and established as a school district for the whole school year, as long as there was at least one student to go to school and one teacher willing to teach at that little school.

That Sherwood School holds special memories of another time, another day. The little one room schoolhouse was built long ago in a large fenced field just off Sherwood Road, atop a rise overlooking grassy rolling meadows bordered by woodlands. Other schoolhouses had been built on this site before the one I attended, and they had burned down. With each rebuilding, various improvements were made, and the schoolhouses became more modern. The earliest listing of a Sherwood Valley School District is the approval of it in 1867. Records show a school building valued at $400.

There was open country on three sides of the field that comprised the school yard. On the fourth side, bordering the schoolyard wire fence, was a small fenced cemetery that served as the final resting place for early pioneer families and American Indian families as well as the current small Sherwood population. The peaceful little tree-shaded cemetery was well tended, and considered sacred ground, and was off-limits for school children. At one time a generous rancher had donated this portion of land for the needs of both the school and the cemetery.

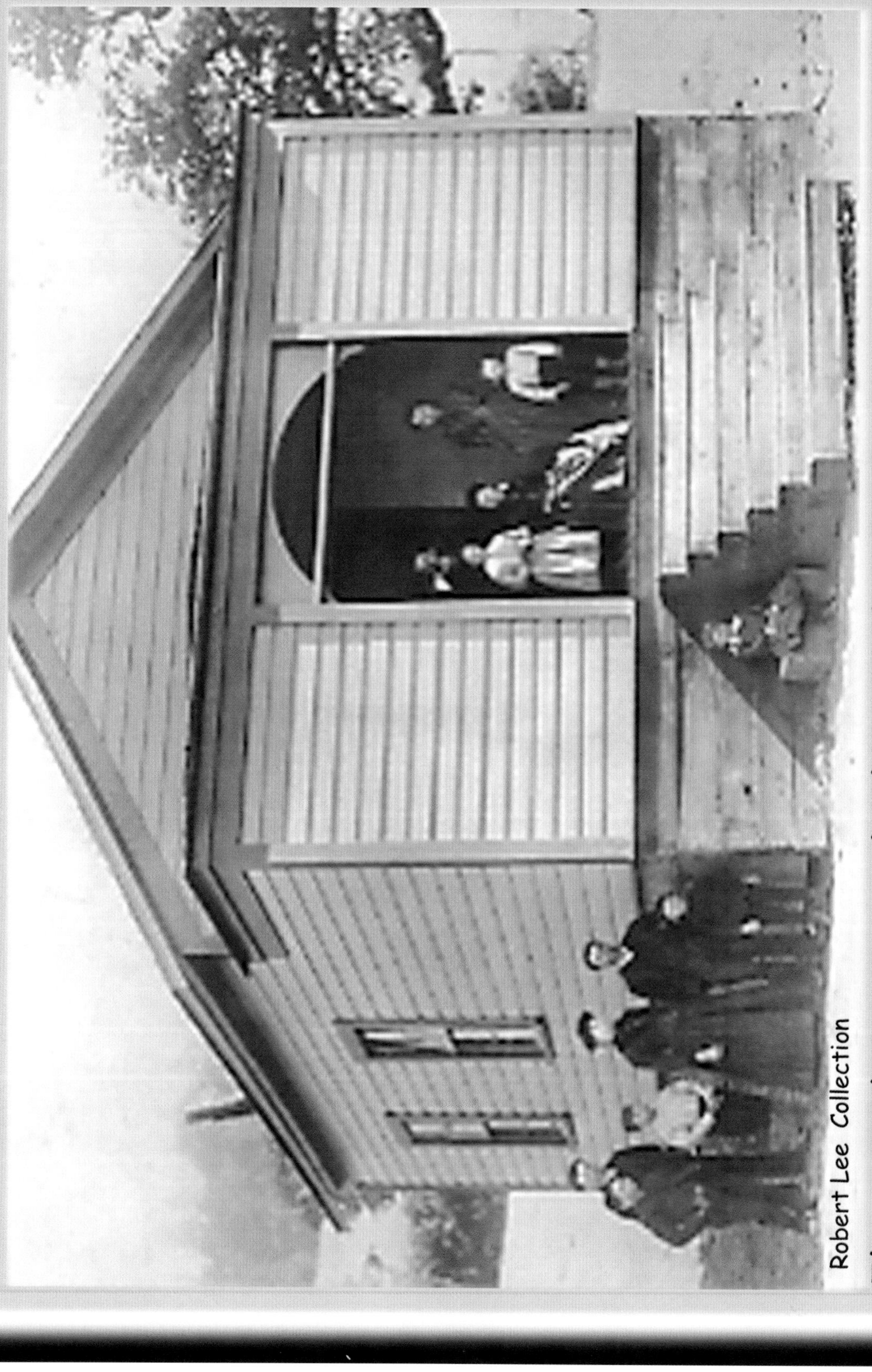


The second one room School House that was built in Sherwood Valley

The outside of the schoolhouse was the classic one-room school in appearance. It was a square wooden building with ship-lap siding, painted white, with a peaked roof, and a sturdy covered front porch with a few steps down to the ground. The sunny south side had a large bank of windows.

The interior of the schoolhouse was light and cheerful with a tall ceiling. The standard framed picture of a serious looking President George Washington graced the wall. There was a large American flag on a pole in the corner by the teacher's desk that we saluted at the beginning of each school day. Another tall wooden flagpole stood outside the school building. The teacher raised the flag on it, first thing each day. If we arrived at school and the flag was not up yet, it usually meant that we got to school ahead of the teacher! We all got to school by different means, by car, by walking, and me sometimes by horseback.

My horse, King, often grew impatient at being tied up all day while I was in school. No matter how well I tied him up, he found a way to get loose. One day I tied him to the heavy three-legged base of the teeter-totter. The teacher, Mrs. Everett, said, "Look out the window". We saw him dragging the heavy teeter-totter base across the yard toward a patch of good looking green grass! The next time he got loose, he broke the reins and headed for home without me. After that, I went back to walking the mile and a half to and from school. It was a pretty walk in the Springtime when the wildflowers began to bloom in all the different little draws and turns along the road. I knew where to look for them, and would pick bouquets to take home to my Mom.

A big, tall parlor stove kept the schoolroom heated. The boys carried wood in for it from the woodshed out in back. The large blackboards all along one wall served the students' needs and had space for the teacher's notes, too. The girls would clean the blackboards and chalk erasers and put out new chalk after each day's lessons. A tall Victrola made of beautiful wood stood in the corner of the room, and was cranked up on special occasions to play a record for us. I remember the unique nostalgic sound of that old music, and hearing the different styles of the recording song artists of that period.

We sat in rows of wooden desks with the fold-up seats, one behind the other. Each desk had a hole on the upper righthand corner to accommodate the jars of ink we used when we wrote with the sharp pointed ink writing pens. We put aside our pencils and used ink for the final copy of composition assignments, and for practicing our penmanship. The rows of desks were mounted one behind the other on long 1"x2"s, and could easily be moved to the edge of the room to accommodate community events and dances.

Held-Poage Collection

Mail Stage in the Sherwood Valley area, the delivery area was very large

The lower grade students sat on the side of the room near the wall with the sunny windows. The upper grade students sat on the other side near the blackboard, which they used a lot more. The older students often helped the younger ones with their studies. There was a large walk-in closet with shelves in back of the teacher's desk where interesting books of all reading levels were kept, even ones on Greek mythology. The closet had a good sized window in it up high, and it was always light and bright. Anyone who finished their lessons and had spare time was welcome to look through them. This closet was also used to keep the school supplies such as paper, scissors, paste, ink, new pencils, and it always smelled good. A cloakroom was across the back of the school-house where the back door went out, and just outside that was the woodshed, kept fully stocked of split wood by the nearby ranching families. Beyond the woodshed was the outhouse, cold in the wintertime, hot in the summertime, but a very necessary fixture.

Outside the sunny south windows, a deep bed of an old fashioned variety of perennial maroon and pink sweet peas thrived and grew up the wall, emitting their wonderful heady fragrance in through the open windows on Spring days. The school's janitor, Stella James, who was the wife of a nearby Sherwood Valley rancher, packed buckets of water to those flowers every year to make them grow. Large silverleaf and cottonwood trees shaded the front yard, and a couple of well used cotton-rope swings hung from their sturdy branches. There were two items of official play equipment in the sideyard, a revolving platform merry-go-round, and a tall giant-strides pole, probably both obtained by local community efforts.

Sherwood school also served as a gathering place for the surrounding residents of the valley. Dances were held there about once a month, with country music being supplied by local talent. The band was made up of three or four people who traded off playing the fiddle, banjo, accordion, guitar, harmonica, and doing the square dance calls. My Mom played the accordion. After a couple of hours of dancing, the band would take a break, and fresh coffee, hot chocolate, fresh milk, and homemade donuts were put out on the cloakroom shelf to tide the crowd over until midnight. This gave everyone a time for visiting and exchanging the news of friends and neighbors. Then the band started playing again, signaling that it was time to get back to the dancing; waltzes, square dances, the Virginia Reel, fox trots, polkas, and The Varsovienne, ("put your little foot, put your little foot, put your little foot right out ....").

At midnight a potluck supper was served by the womenfolk who saw to it that everyone was well fed. Then usually the dancing went on until dawn when it was time to go home to milk the cows and feed the chickens. Usually we children got to stay up for the hot chocolate and donuts, and sometimes we even got to stay up as late as the

Jani Buron Collection

1945 Chet Griffith's six horse "Home Stretch Van". Chet hauled Howard horses

midnight feed! Then we were put to bed in the family car amid soft quilts and pillows. We could hear the soft sweet strains of the fiddles and accordion music floating through the night air as we drifted off to sleep.

Eventually Dad did leave Willowbrook and began driving the horse van full time on long hauls. Mom stayed to finish teaching the school year out at Sherwood school, and I finished out the fourth grade there that year. After we moved off the Willowbrook Ranch, Mom and John and I boarded with nearby farm families in Sherwood until school was out for the summer. The first family we stayed with was Charley Anderson, a logger, and his wife, Bev, who lived near the school.

The next family we stayed with had a ranch a few miles down the road toward Willits. A diminutive older woman, Piney, and her nephew, Jerry, farmed the place, and lived in the old ranch house with small dark rooms. We carried wood in for the wood cook stove and the heating stove, and helped them with their other chores. The wood heater was fired up to warm the room where we took our bath in a large washtub a couple of times a week. Piney was a character, and I remember how her eyes twinkled when she told us stories of other times. She had a pleasant happy laugh. Jerry was fairly serious and was always busy fixing things on the ranch. They both worked hard taking care of their place.

John Bosko Collection

Ray Kane the foreman of Ridgewood Ranch during the early 1940's with Seabiscuit

# Chapter 3

## RETURN TO RIDGEWOOD

When the Sherwood school year was over, and Dad was still hauling horses, Mom went with him sometimes to help drive. During this time I went to live with the Jones Family in their comfortable old ranch house on Ridgewood Ranch. I stayed there that summer and started school with the girls in Willits that fall of 1946. Mom and my little brother stayed in Willits. Dad, Mom, John and I all got together often for visits. Dad stayed in touch with Ray Kane, who was the foreman of C. S. Howard's Ridgewood Ranch at that time. Mr. Howard had brought his famous horse, Seabiscuit, home to retire when Dad worked there the first time. Now that World War II was over, and gas rationing was a thing of the past, Mr. Howard was building up a breeding farm with beautiful hand-picked mares. He had other studs there, too, and he still kept his racing stable active.

Dad and Ray had been friends for a long time, since their earlier rodeo cowboy days together. Eventually, Mr. Howard asked my Dad to come back to work for him a second time, this time as foreman of the Thoroughbred horses on the ranch, mostly to look after the fine broodmares. Dad liked the idea of working with Ray, and being around the Thoroughbred horses. Eventually we all were back at Ridgewood. And Seabiscuit was there! That wonderful champion of a horse who had run and won and set track records all over the country.

When Mr. Howard was asking my Dad about coming back to work on his Ridgewood Ranch, Dad hesitated a little while thinking about it. Mr. Howard threw in some extra incentive: he said that he would build us a new house if we came back! He would build it like my folks wanted, the newest and the most modern, whatever suited them. My Mom said "Yes!" I don't know if my Dad ever had a chance to say aye, yes, or no! Mr. Howard and my Dad were good friends, that was a plus, and Dad liked everything about Ridgewood Ranch. Mom and I said it was wonderful. My brother was just toddler age, and he always liked it there. It was a good move.

Our new house would be built right on the crest of the hill overlooking the lower hay fields and the pear orchard and the Redwood grove. This would be on the exact spot where the old house was that the Jones Family lived in when I stayed with them. They planned to dismantle the old house after the Jones family moved down to a larger two-story house at the main headquarters compound.

John Bosko Collection

Mr. Howard riding Seabiscuit with western saddle at Ridgewood Ranch

Building us a new house was right in line with Mr. Howard's thoughtful ways. C. S. Howard's generosity was well known throughout all the communities that he was a part of. The people that were employed by him and those who were associated with him in other ways were all aware of his kind gestures, usually done quietly and without fanfare. Ernie Banker of Ukiah remembers well that Howard's considerations were timely and generous.

As a young man in the early 1930's, Ernie's father, Floyd Banker, owned a Buick dealership in Ukiah, California, for Charles Howard. His dealership did well, and Howard offered Floyd a position as a sales manager in his San Francisco location. Floyd thought about moving to the City, and then laughingly asked, "Do you suppose they would let me go deer hunting in Golden Gate Park?" He stayed on in Ukiah.

Ernie recalls his Dad taking him deer hunting on Ridgewood Ranch with Mr. Howard when he was very young. His Dad woke him up early in the morning so they could go have breakfast with the ranch hands and the cowboys before going hunting. Ernie was amazed at the full ranch style breakfast served of steak, ham, bacon, potatoes, hotcakes, biscuits and eggs. He asked his Dad why they ate such a big breakfast, and his Dad told him, "The ones who are going out riding all day will take only that little pile of jerky with them that is sitting in front of their plate. They won't have anything else to eat all day until they get back to the cookhouse tonight. So they are eating hearty now!"

Floyd was married and had a family, and the time came when he wanted to build a small house in the town of Ukiah. Floyd's Buick dealership was doing well, and he borrowed money from Howard to build a two-bedroom home. Floyd moved his family into the new home. A while later, Floyd found that he needed surgery to repair a painful hernia condition. He made an appointment with a San Francisco hospital to get this done, but they postponed his surgery because of a hospital emergency. He decided to get the surgery done locally. Due to complications from the surgery, Floyd died shortly after, at the age of 30, leaving his wife and children with a new home to be paid off. They had been in the home for less than a year.

The widowed Mrs. Banker got enough money together to send a house payment to Mr. Howard. Within a short time, she received a letter back from him with her uncashed payment check in it, along with the ownership deed to their Ukiah house! Mr. Howard had marked the loan "paid in full", and had given the Banker family their home, free and clear. Such generosity was not common, although it was Mr. Howard's way. Mrs. Banker was, of course, grateful. Not knowing what to do, she took the letter and deed to a consultant to ask what to do next. He said, "Go cash your check, and record the deed to your house, right now!"

Ernie graduated from Ukiah High School in 1939, and then took a pilot training program in Junior College. He was interested in all kinds of airplanes. One Sunday when he heard about a P-36 airplane that had crashed near Sebastopol, he decided to get in some flying time that day and fly over the crash site to have a look. He had rented his 40-horsepower Cub from the airport for one hour, and after viewing the P-36 crash, he continued to fly until that hour was up. As he approached the Santa Rosa Airport landing strip, he noticed some men standing on the runway, which was unusual. He landed, and two of the men approached his plane and reached up and put their hands on the wingtips of his plane. He asked why, and one of them said, "We were waiting for you. You are the last plane down on this Santa Rosa runway today, and we wanted to be sure that you didn't take off again. All airports across the country are closed down now, because Pearl Harbor was bombed by Japan this morning." Ernie later went into the service. He was based in Italy and the South of France, where he flew 50 missions.

Ernie's mother, Mrs. Banker, kept ownership of the house that Mr. Howard gave them for many years. When she moved, she rented the house out. In her later years, she lived in the Palace Hotel, and eventually she sold the house to the man who owned the hotel.

The Jones Family I lived with at Ridgewood in 1946 had two daughters, Laverne and Betty, both just older than me, and an older son, Hubert. The girls and I were friends, and their parents, Curley and Verna, made me feel at home, and what fun we had! We three girls rode, swam, hiked, and explored and played all over that ranch. Their folks took us to town in Willits for the Saturday afternoon movies at the Noyo Theater, Westerns, of course! We knew all the cowboy stars and their horses by name. After the movies, when we were going home from Willits all the way back down the twisty grade to Ridgewood, we had a tradition of singing favorite songs, back to back, all the way home. Curley and Verna, sitting in the front seat, usually sang their special version of "Let The Rest of The World Go By" on these evenings.

Betty and Laverne's parents allowed us to stay up late on Friday and Saturday nights, since there was no school the next day. One of our favorite pastimes on those evenings was to lie on the living room floor with our ears pressed to the little radio so we could listen to the late-night mystery shows: The Shadow, ("Only The Shadow knows...."), The Phantom, Superman, Mystery Theater, Spiderman, and the latest and scariest one of all, Inner Sanctum, opening with the sound of the famous squeaking door. By the time Inner Sanctum came around late at night, we really had ourselves spooked and jumpy! We had our coloring books and crayons spread out on the floor between us so we could color while we listened to the programs.

One evening while we were listening to mysteries, and coloring, as usual, that old house on the hill that we lived in began to creak and squeak and it seemed like it was moving around with a life of its own. Then a quick, jerky jolt, followed by some minor trembling and shaking. Lying on our bellies on the floor while quietly listening to the radio late at night, we really felt the movement. Our first wide-eyed thought was that this happening was somehow connected to the mystery programs we were listening to. Maybe the boogey-man ghost was really coming here! Or maybe the older brother Hubert was playing some kind of a joke on us ... no, he wasn't home right now ... We didn't know what was going on, but it woke the folks up, too, and we three scrambled up off the floor and went running into their bedroom fast! They said it was an earthquake, and they knew that for sure, it wouldn't hurt us any, and for us to turn the radio spook shows off and go to bed. And go to sleep. Now! That was my first earthquake, and what a scary time to happen, during the late night mystery programs! We did go right to bed, with no more mystery programs that night! We had all the fright we needed for one evening!

The Jones Family house was an old ranch house perched on the edge of a hill, and it had a large screen porch where we kids all slept in the summertime. In the winter, we slept inside in a very small room, with just room enough for our three single beds against the walls, and a narrow walkway around them. The inside walls were unfinished, and the vertical 2x4's were exposed. Someone had nailed short horizontal 2x4's in between the uprights, and they served as shelves to display Laverne and Betty's impressive collection of horse and dog figurines. The large screen porch had several steps down to the grassy front yard. On nice mornings, Laverne and I sat out there on the steps while she combed my mass of curly hair into place before we left for school. She was like my big sister, helping me whenever I needed it.

At night, when we girls were in our beds, the car headlights from the Ridgewood Grade would shine on our bedroom wall as the cars went in and out of the turns going up and down the highway. The lights came in through the little squares of glass in the sliding wooden-pane windows, creating a dancing light show in our bedroom. Sometimes while lying on our bed, we would put our bare feet up on the wall and let the lights dance across our toes. We could also hear the sound of the screeching car brakes going around each turn on the grade. We imagined all kinds of things about the cars traveling down the grade ... "hear that screech?"... "I don't see anymore lights"... "I know that one went off the edge!" One time we heard an especially loud screech noise, ending in what we imagined to be a crash into the guardrail, and then more crashing noises like something was tumbling downhill. We all got up and ran into the folks bedroom and told them what we had just heard, each of us describing a different sound. They said it was probably our runaway imaginations, and to go back to bed and go to sleep.

We did hear later of a car wreck on the Grade, and a traveling salesman who had been missing for a long time. Someone said his car was eventually found at the bottom of the canyon, where it probably still is. It was up for argument if he was found in it, or was thrown out, or if his poor dried up remains were ever discovered.

In the summertime, we helped the girls' mom, Verna, pick blackberries from the lush vines that grew along the creek. Our efforts always paid off when Verna made us a blackberry pie or cobbler. Wherever we went blackberry picking, we also played under the huge, overhanging vines, pretending to be the little rabbits that had their burrows in the thick brush there.

We had cute little kittens we played with, and since they wouldn't follow us like the dogs did, we would put a leash on them and take them to the creek for swimming lessons. Poor kittens. We were just trying to cool them off. We didn't know then how much cats disliked water, even on a hot day! The dogs went swimming freely, and loved the water. But the kitties didn't care how hot the summer got, they did not feel the need to go in the water!

Occasionally we would ride out to the main entrance gate on Highway 101 and ride the inside trail along the split-rail fence by the road to watch the cars going by. We had different games we made up about who could call the car colors first, and the make of each car, and the state on the license plate. There were not as many makes and models of cars then as there are now, and this made it easy to recognize the distinctive shapes of all kinds of car makes from quite a distance. The passengers in those cars going by us were usually pleased to see riders on horseback, especially the city tourists who drove up the Redwood Highway 101 to the country in the summertime.

Hubert Jones, Laverne and Betty's big brother, was lightweight and had a slight build when he was young. Mr. Howard asked him to exercise the horses around the ranch, and to try his hand at breaking the colts. He was strong enough to hold the horses under control, and he was also light weight enough to be a jockey. Mr. Howard observed Hubert's improving horsemenship and asked him to come to the racetrack to ride for the Howard Racing Stables. Mr. Howard made a good choice picking Hubert to be one of his jockeys. Hubert won lots of big races and he wore the Howard silks proudly. He was riding at the same time as George Woolf. Being a jockey and riding at the different racetracks took him away from his Ridgewood home a lot. We heard from him from time to time, which always made his Dad and Mom happy.

Jones Family Collection

George Woolf & Hubert Jones, Belmont Park 1944

Jones Family Collection

Hubert Jones on a Howard colt out of his prize mare, Sag Rock

1950

Trainer

Chet Griffith

with a winner

On the left:

Iny Griffith one

of the ground crew

at a Ridgewood

branding

Chet and Iny Griffith are parents of author Jani Buron

We went down to meet Hubert at the Pleasanton Racetrack one time to bring him home. It was quite a long ride in the Jones Family car along old Highway 101 when it was a two-lane highway that went through all the little towns. It was my first trip to that town, and I hadn't seen a racetrack before. Later, unbeknownst to me then, my family would move from Ridgewood Ranch to that very town, where my Dad would begin his career training racehorses. It was then that I learned about the excitement and wonder of the world of the racing Thoroughbreds. Seabiscuit had been here, and at many other tracks, and he knew all about running and competing with other horses. I would not realize until later what it took to be a champion like Seabiscuit certainly was. All I knew then was ranching and rodeo... racing was still to come. I knew that Seabiscuit had been a great racehorse, and yet he was so calm and friendly to us at the ranch, and was my favorite of all the Howard horses. I did not understand until many years later about the difficulties that Seabiscuit had overcome to win his races and become the public's idol.He captured as much attention as any movie star ever did.

Pleasanton was a nice little country town then, mostly a rancher's, horseman's, and dairyman's family-type community. The center of town had three or four restaurants, The Rose Hotel, Christensen's Tack Room, a couple of bars and a pool room, a couple of gas stations, and a post office. The elementary school was at the south end of town, and the high school was at the north end. Before we left town, we went by to visit a couple of families that the Joneses' knew. One of those families were the Fergusons, and I came to know them very well later at the racetrack.

We took Hubert home to Ridgewood, where he stayed for a little while, and then he left again to go back to riding races. While Hubert was home, he would do special things for us girls if he had time. He hiked up Big Rock Candy Mountain with us to help us put up a flag that would stay up! We had installed several white flags on top of that rock, but they usually got knocked over by the wild goats or the winter winds. Hubert brought wire, nails, screws, and a hammer. He put a short stout flagpole up for us that lasted for years. After that, we just had to replace the flag when it was worn out.

When it was time to tear down the old ranch house that the Jones Family and I lived in, so the new Griffith Family house could be built on that site, the Jonses, and I with them, moved down to the two-story ranch house at the main headquarters compound. This much larger house was one of the first ones built on this ranch in the mid-1800's. A single story cookhouse was attached to the West end of the big two-story house.

This house had a whole different spacious feel to it, and each of us girls had our own upstairs bedroom! This was quite a contrast to having our three single beds crowded

Curley Jones riding Seabiscuit

Jones Family collection

Verna Jones getting ready for a roundup picnic at Ridgewood

Jani Buron Collection

Above are the parents of Hubert Jones, Laverne Booth, Betty Peters

into that one small bedroom in the old house. Curley and Verna had their bedroom downstairs. I lived there with the Joneses' until my own family came down to the ranch, and we four temporarily moved into the upstairs living quarters in the Upper Mare Barn. Marcela Howard had arranged to have that apartment remodeled for us. We lived there until our new house on the hill was completed. I always felt at home on Ridgewood Ranch, whatever house I lived in.

We three girls rode everywhere on that Ranch, with strict orders to "not ride off the ranch!" from each of our parents. With 17,000 acres at our disposal, we had plenty of places to explore. But we knew where the property lines of the Ranch were, and we didn't go off unless we asked our folks first.

## THE RIDE TO PAYNE'S PLACE

With special permission from our folks, we could go on "all day rides" to visit neighboring ranch families. These were great adventures for us, and we always dutifully checked in with the destination family. The agreement with our folks was that we would turn around and start back home at noon, when the sun was directly overhead, no matter where we were, thus assuring our safe return back to the home barn with plenty of daylight to spare. We would take a lunch and treats, and drink water from the little clear running creeks along the way. We three girls did so enjoy the adventure of the long rides into new territory. One of these rides that I remember especially well was a ride where we planned to go north from Ridgewood to see the Payne Family who lived on Hwy 101 just south of Willits. We went to school with their two boys, Billy and Bobby. Their Dad, Al, shod all the horses at Ridgewood.

I can still picture Al Payne's blacksmith shop at Ridgewood, and can recall the dominating smell of the freshly trimmed horse hooves. There was also the smell of hot iron in the air, and a mixture of horse and human sweat. The coal in the hot forge fire had its own peculiar musty odor. I can still hear the steamy hissssssing and crackle sound of the hot horse shoes being lowered into the water to cool off and set the shape. The pungent smell of the iodine, Pine Tar, Butter of Antimony, and other mixtures being applied to keep the horses hooves pliable and healthy, always hung in the air. When the blacksmith was shaping the hot shoes on the anvil with heavy iron tools, it produced a musical, rhythmic sound of iron pounding on iron that rang out across the ranch compound. The ranch dogs waited around the blacksmith shop patiently for a chance to grab up the hoof trimmings before they were swept up from the wooden floor. They savored those trimmings; to them it was better than bones or steak. They chewed on them, licked them, and eventually ate them up.

Al Payne shod all of the saddle horses, all the work horses, and a few of the Thoroughbreds that needed it and, of course, Seabiscuit, because Charles and Marcela rode him around the ranch. Al seemed to work tirelessly to get all the horses done. The blacksmith shop was his kingdom, and he had the final say of everything in there. If it was your horse's day to get shod, you better get him over there at the appointed time!

The day came when the weather was just right, and so we asked permission from our folks to do the all day ride to Payne's place. The back trail north to their place was a fun ride, although rugged, and we felt it was kind of remote, wild and adventuresome. The older Jones girl, Laverne, chose to ride a young green mare, and get some trail time in on her. The mare was still a little skittish, and had some trail lessons to learn, and Laverne was a good hand for this. The mare was named Honey because of her pretty honey-colored flaxen mane and tail. Betty rode Charro, Laverne's big black horse Hubert got for her from a ranch in Colorado.

I rode one of the ranch horses named Tick Tock, a big , black and white paint lead-horse from the track, who, by the way, had his own ideas about behavior. He had been a pony horse for Mr. Howard's racing stable, and had taken Seabiscuit to the track many times. He was also used to accompany Seabiscuit around the ranch during 'Biscuit's recovery time before he went back to win the "Hundred Grander" (Santa Anita Handicap) on his third try. Tick Tock was a good stout trail horse, and could probably ride all day and never get tired. Might get crabby if he missed a meal, but never tired.

The ride to Payne's place went just fine. It was a pretty day, and the trail was clear, just like the last time we had come this way. We rested and watered our horses at Payne's while we visited with the family and ate our lunch. We talked about the big old barn in the meadow that had the large painted advertisements on each barn wall facing the highway ... "Mail Pouch Tobacco" ... "Dr. Pierce's Fine Liniment". It even had an advertisement painted on the roof for airplane occupants to see as they flew over! The big barn with its colorful ads dominated the scenery in that meadow for many years. It had stood for a long time before it got tired, and began to slowly buckle and then finally collapsed into the earth.

After lunch, we said our good-byes to the Paynes and then started our return trip. We found that we were going back down the trail to Ridgewood a little later than we had planned. We hurriedly rode across the field and back to the trail, then on over the ridge and on down the other side of the hill toward home. No dilly-dallying on this return trip. Tick Tock became impatient at being hurried, I guess, and probably thought he was

Still girls after 52 years apart

They met at Ridgewood in 2002

Big Rock Candy Mountain

Jani Buron Collection

Left: Betty, Center: Jani, Right: Laverne

hungry again. We were riding single file on the trail with Betty in front, me in the middle, and Laverne in back, all of us moving right along in an effort to get back home on time.

About an hour into the return ride, we were going along the trail through some brushy country with a few little clearings here and there. We came out of the brush into a very small clearing, and just as Betty rode across it and went back into the brush ahead of me, I entered the clearing. At that point, I felt Tick Tock draw the reins quickly through my fingers, faster than I could stop them. I quickly glanced down, and Tick Tock pulled his head down so fast, and this time it was not to grab at a mouthful of grass. He wanted to buck. I tugged hard on the reins, trying to pull his head up to stop him, but I was not strong enough. He was going into action, and I couldn't hold him back. Tick Tock let loose with all he had. I felt like I was riding a saddle bronc in a rodeo! He crowhopped, then he bucked, and I could hear Betty and Laverne yelling at me to stay on, and to pull his head around tight one way to stop his bucking. Well, try pulling his head around; he didn't even know I was pulling on the rein with all the strength a ten year old girl has!

Tick Tock's first jump, a crowhop, caught me by surprise! His second jump, when he really started bucking, I daylighted the saddle, and came back down hard. Halfway through the third jump, he threw me way high in the air. I was off, going up, and up ... then I was coming down to meet the hard rocky ground of the sidehill, flat on my back. I hit hard and, of course, it knocked the wind out of me. It actually knocked me out cold for a minute or two.

Betty and Laverne quickly dismounted and caught up Tick Tock, who had quit bucking as soon as I was off and had gone to eating some of the select little bunches of grass that grew in the clearing. Then they rushed over to me and bent over my prone form to check out my condition. After I woke up, and quit gasping for air, and I knew where I was, lying there looking up at the sky, the girls helped me up. Then I realized that my ankle was painfully injured. I could hardly put any weight on it. We didn't know if it was broken, but it sure felt like it.

The girls made a quick plan; Laverne would take Charro, the fastest traveling horse, and go back to the ranch to get help. She would tell our parents that Betty and I would be coming in later than planned and explain about Tick Tock's misbehavior, and just what happened on the trail on the way back. Betty would take Tick Tock. In case he had any more ideas about bucking, she would be in better shape to handle him than I would be. That left me the green mare, Honey, who had really behaved rather nicely the whole journey. Laverne said she thought the mare was too tired to be any problem. Then she took a shorter trail back to the Ranch, and Betty and I took a longer, easier trail back.

I didn't feel like getting back on right away, so I led Honey the rest of the way down the hill, me hobbling like a crippled chicken, and she patiently staying beside me. I think she kind of understood the scope of the situation.

Then we came to the fields where some Hereford cow-calf pairs were grazing. The herd cows with calves didn't look entirely friendly, and the closer we got to them, the harder they glared at us. Mama cows can be very grouchy when it comes to anyone disturbing their babies. I quickly found a place on the fence where I could climb up on the mare, feeling safer on horseback. She was a nice riding mare, and yes, she was tired, too. We rode on past the cows without further incident, except for the Mama cows glaring at us to make sure we were continuing to ride on past them.

It was getting on into evening, even maybe dark time. I was getting tired, something that usually didn't happen to me whenever I was riding. But the ankle pain, scrapes and bruises, and sore muscles from my wreck were beginning to get my attention. What concerned us even more was that our folks would want to put a stop to our long wonderful rides because of this accident. And why had Tick Tock bucked? Did he get a burr or a bee under his blanket, or was he just tired of being ridden all day, or hungry for some green grass, or just ornery? We never knew. I rode him again often, without any more bucking incidents.

Betty and I rode on, talking softly into the night air. We were following the fenceline trail down out of the hills into the flat land, a bit weary, and glad to be getting closer to the main part of the Ranch, and home. As we were riding along in the early twilight, we were surprised to see a pair of car headlights off in the distance. The car was slowly coming across the bumpy plowed field toward us, its headlights going up and down and this way and that over the rough ground. We knew there wasn't any road where that car was travelling. After all that had happened that day, we didn't know what to expect now. Then we heard familiar voices. What a relief! It was Hubert driving the Jones Family car slowly across the field, and Laverne beside the car on horseback, leading the way back to the trail where she expected to see Betty and me coming out of the hills. Betty called out to them. Laverne could see us in the twilight, then she pointed the way for the car.

My Mom was there in the car, too, worried, of course, having only heard part of the story before she saw us. They got near us and stopped the car. Someone helped me off the mare, although I said I was willing to ride her back to the barn and put her away. We always put our own horses away and fed them after riding. Someone else said, "Enough riding for today, let's see how you are. Get in the car, and we'll put your horse away." Hubert rode the mare back and put her away, and I rode home in the car, and explained the whole story to the folks.

When we got back to the house, my Mom and Dad examined my ankle, swollen and twisted, but not terribly bruised. They got a bucket of warm water and Epsom Salts for me to soak my foot in. We didn't go to the doctor, the nearest one being Doc Babcock in Willits, as it was quite a trip to town. They decided that rest would help it. The best thing was that no one said our little accident should bring a stop to our riding in the hills. They seemed to think that these things happen every now and then, and just chalk it up to experience!

It was a long time until I walked straight on my ankle, because it hurt when I did. I kind of walked on my outer foot with my toes twisted inward. One day my Mom said, "Enough of you walking like that, it is time you put your foot down and walk flat!" I forced my foot flat, and it hurt, but eventually it got back to normal. And it never did stop me from riding!

Another place we rode to once in a while was the Soda Spring, located north of the Upper Mare Barn. We always took some empty bottles to fill and bring back home. This spring bubbled out from the bottom of a round, fairly bare hillside, and ran for a little ways on top of the ground. The bubbly water tasted like soda water and mineral water, combined, and it left orange-colored deposits on the rocks where it came out of the hill. What we took home in bottles never tasted quite the same later on, as it had when it was fresh out of the spring. On the way to the Soda Spring, there was an interesting place right by the road across the fence that had three large indented circles in the ground. They were very evenly round, and one was larger than the others. Someone said they were Indian teepee circles, and that seemed like it could be right. We found arrowheads there. We had quite a time playing games, each of us having one of those indented circles for our own play house.

## UPPER MARE BARN APARTMENT

Back to the circumstances that brought us to live at Ridgewood ... the new house sounded great to my Mom ... Dad loved his job with the horses ... I loved having that entire place to ride! My brother didn't have much to say, he was just a little guy, and he went where we went.

While our new house was being built, we lived in the long, narrow, two-bedroom apartment in the loft of the big Upper Mare Barn. This barn was located at the far north end of the ranch complex where the livestock scales were, and where the marking and brandings took place in later years. An identical ranchhand apartment was also built in the south end of the barn. This barn had many tall pine trees and spreading oak trees around it that provided shade for the corrals and runways.

This Upper Mare Barn was located at the end of the road that went past the Stud Barn where Seabiscuit and the other Howard stallions were kept and was quite a ways from the main ranch headquarters. The upstairs apartment was a comfortable place, although small, in a kind of an "A" frame configuration. The other mare barn, known as the Lower Mare Barn, was at the south end of the main ranch headquarters where the foaling operations took place. The barn floor plans were identical, with the Lower Mare Barn having a few more stalls and it was configured to accommodate the birthing of the new Thoroughbred foals. The shedrows in both barns were wide and spacious, and the inside corners of the barn were gracefully rounded. They were both beautiful, well built barns, with all the latest and most modern applications that Mr. Howard found available to put in them. He spared no expense when it came to making his horses comfortable and well cared for.

The young horses being broke to ride were brought to the Upper Mare Barn where the men handled them and got them used to a saddle and to being ridden. I remember seeing Hubert coaxing young colts into compliance, and climbing on their backs and riding them until they stopped bucking. Upstairs, where we lived, you could hear the horses soft sounds at night as they moved around in their stalls, and an occasional soft nicker, or even a whinny. The delightful fragrance of the fresh straw and healthy horseflesh drifted up the long stairway to our apartment. I felt so close to the horses; we were all bedding down in the same building, each in our own quarters.

While we lived in the barn, our cousins would come to visit, and they thought this was the greatest place to play! Being there right close to the horses, and having all the hay to play in, and the barn to run around in was something they really enjoyed. Later when we moved into our new house and the families came to visit, the cousins asked if we could go back over to that barn and play hide-and-seek again!

At the edge of the barnyard between the Buggy Horse Barn and the Upper Mare Barn stood a large old hay barn. Looking south from there across a small draw was the backside of the Howards' large saddle horse barn, the carriage house, the Big House with its lush gardens, and the gardener's cottage, where Norman the English Gardener lived. Looking west from here across one of the creeks that ran through the ranch, you could see the knoll where our new house was being built. To get to the new house by road, it was a long way around past the Stud Barn and on down through the ranch headquarters, then back onto the road past the slaughter house and over the bridge that went up to Walker Lake. But we used a shortcut when we were on foot or horseback by going on a trail down from the hay barn and then cutting through the fields and finding a crossing on the creek, and then up the hill to our new house in no time!

## OLD BUGGY HORSE RACING BARN

Near the Upper Mare Barn and across the maze of large and small corrals, there was an old low-roofed barn called "The Racing Barn". We were told that buggy horses had once been kept there. We also knew that Seabiscuit had his temporary quarters there when he came home to Ridgewood in 1939 to heal up from his racing injuries. It was not known then if he would ever race again. The security was very tight, with someone being near Seabiscuit at all times. He seemed to be very fond of his new quarters, and was happy to be at Ridgewood with the Howards and all the other horses and animals. He was curious about his new surroundings, and he looked at and sniffed everything to get acquainted. He was royalty, like the King of the Ranch, but he was unaware of his status. He preferred to be very low profile royalty.

Upon investigating the Racing Barn several years after Seabiscuit had been stabled there, when it was empty, we three girls found shelves with lots of containers of good strong smelling horse medicine of another era, and small brushes for applying medicines to horses' legs. We found it intriguing to mix up new solutions and witches brews with all that stuff. What goo! What thick, black, strong smelling glorious goo! We were told later that the barn was off limits to us. Somehow, the grown-ups could tell that we had been there! But we found that old place irresistible, and did return now and then, but we were very careful to cover our tracks, and not do harm to anything or leave anything out of place. The barn just held such a fascination for us with all its stalls and runways and rooms with little square wooden pane windows. A narrow stairway led to a small lookout room above the barn roof, where a watchman sometimes stayed, and you could see in all directions from here. Mr. Howard was very thorough on the security for the people and animals and everything on the Ranch, and the watchman could see a lot from this little lookout room.

We found the ancient leather buggy-horse harness hanging neatly on the walls to be very interesting. That harness brought many questions to our minds, since we had never seen a harness-horse race. We imagined what kind of horses used to occupy that different kind of barn, and where they were stalled, and where they ate. In our childhood games, we pretended we were those horses of long ago, being harnessed up and pulling the two-wheeled racing buggies.

## HOWARD HOSPITAL, DOC BABCOCK, JOHN & LADDIE, RIDGEWOOD GRADE

When we were living at the Upper Mare Barn apartment, one evening my little brother, John, then a toddler, was quietly playing near me in our bedroom as I was lying on my bed reading. My old Cocker Spaniel dog, Laddie, was napping on the floor in there, too. Somehow, John brushed up against the very sore ears of the old dog. The dog was startled, yelped with pain and turned with his mouth open, and John, being on the same face to face level as the dog, was badly bitten across the nose. Immediately there was lots of screaming, the baby was crying, his face was bleeding, and the dog was yelping in confusion and pain.

Mom came running into the room screaming, "What happened?" Then when she saw John had been injured, her voice went up a notch, and she shouted, "What are we going to do?!". She quickly grabbed blankets and wrapped the baby up and started for the door. Dad grabbed the offending dog, kicked him, and threw him into a side-wall closet, then yelled at me to get my jacket and get downstairs and into the car quick because we're going to Doc Babcock at the hospital in Willits.

Everyone moved fast, getting downstairs and into the car, even though we were numbed, not knowing what damage had been done to my brother's face or to his eye. He was bleeding too much to see where the actual injury was. We had a long way to go to the Howard Hospital in Willits and Doc Babcock. Dad started the car and we quickly wound our way on down the dirt ranch road from the Upper Mare Barn past the Stud Barn and to the main ranch gate. Once there, we turned north on Highway 101, and started uphill where our headlights shone onto the long, twisting two lane highway north up Ridgewood Grade.

It seemed to take forever to drive to Willits. Mom was crying, John was hurt, Dad was absolutely silent, except for an occasional brief answer to one of Mom's hysterical questions. Dad's attention was on driving that Chevy sedan hard to make the fastest trip possible up the mountain highway to the hospital. I was in the back seat, curled up, also silent, and frightened. I was hoping and praying that my baby brother would be OK.

The northbound uphill right-hand lane of the Ridgewood Grade pressed against a vertical sheer rocky bank. The thin white line down the center divided it from the outside lane, which was southbound and, of course, downhill. That outside lane twisted along the two-foot high, dented and scraped guardrail that marked the outer edge of the narrow highway pavement. Many a vehicle had hit or leaned against that guardrail when going around a turn too fast, or if the conditions were icy and had sent them skidding into it.

That low white guardrail was the only thing between your car and the top of a long sheer drop down into the brushy canyon below. Several cars now rested down in that canyon permanently because it would be extremely difficult to retrieve them. From the passenger side of the car when travelling southbound in that outside lane, one got quite a view straight down into the gaping, narrow canyon that seemed so dark at the bottom, even in the daytime. It was a treacherous enough highway in the daytime, and at night and in a hurry when you were scared, like now, it was even worse.

Up that grade we went, then across the summit past the Howard Forestry Hill, then on down the road into the south end of Willits. Dad got to the Howard Hospital driveway entrance, and made the sharp left turn off the highway and drove quickly up the steep hill to the hospital. All in one motion he quickly parked, pulled the brake, jumped out and went around the other side of the car to help Mom with my brother, and told me to stay in the car, don't go anywhere, and he'd be back for me. I knew he would be.

It seemed that during that waiting time, for me, the clock had stopped. Nothing but semidarkness, quiet, and me in the car, waiting for Dad to come back. I could see into the lighted rooms of the hospital windows. I saw nurses rushing around in the emergency room to tend to my brother's needs. Once in a while I got a glimpse of Dad or Mom.

Doc Babcock was summoned quickly to assess the damages, and to stitch up the face of this little boy that he had delivered in a complicated birth just a couple of years earlier. At one point, after Doc got the bleeding stopped on John's face, and got control of the present situation, he happened to glance up at my Dad who was helping to hold John still. Doc noticed my Dad's pale color, and the woozy look in his eye. He said, with a chuckle, "Chet, get out of here, I don't need two of you down flat!" So after all the cut-up and injured horses and other animals my Dad had patched up without a problem, he now found it was somewhat different when it was his own baby that was injured!

While waiting out in the car, my thoughts went back to when Doc Babcock had saved my Dad's life one time. This was before my brother was born when we lived at Willowbrook Ranch. A large Belgian workmare had gone berserk and turned on Dad when they were inoculating the horses for sleeping sickness. She got scared, and she knocked him down and trampled him repeatedly, front and back. The ranchhands then brought him

Jani Buron Collection

Jani with brother John, dog Laddie and Billy the Kid

Above, Jani and little brother John going for a ride at Ridgewood.
The house was occupied by many ranch families.
Below left, Young John and Laddie becoming friends again.
Below right, Jani and John's parents, Chet and Iny Griffith.

in to Willits all the way down the ten miles of narrow bumpy mountain road to Howard Hospital, expecting that he had fatal injuries.

We were living in Laytonville when word came to us that Dad had been hurt in that bad accident with the work mare at Willowbrook. We rushed down to Willits, and I remember seeing him in the hospital. He had a pattern of huge hoofprints of broken skin that walked up his chest, to his head, and down his back. Doc Babcock said we could go in and visit with him for awhile. Dad was sure glad to see us. He even managed a faint smile in spite of his extreme discomfort. I was about as tall as where Dad's face lay on the high hospital bed, so we were about face to face. When Mom stepped out of the room to talk to Doc, Dad opened his eyes a little and spoke softly to me, saying he was OK, and that everything was going to be all right, and not to worry. His words, even though spoken in a halting manner, made me feel so much better, and made me think that what I saw was not as bad as it really was. Indeed, his injuries were very serious.

I wanted to stay in there with Dad, but we were whisked out quickly when Doc Babcock and the nurses came in to work on him some more. Doc examined him again, and told us that it was important that he lie very quietly until his wounds began to heal. He also had a serious concussion to the head. With a little time to heal up, Dad made it through OK, thanks to Doc's wise decisions on his immediate treatment. Doc told us later that Dad most likely wouldn't have survived the trampling if he wasn't such a hard-headed Irishman! We all had a good-natured laugh about that. We were sure glad that hospital was there, thanks to Mr. Howard's efforts. Doc Babcock was as much a hero to me as Seabiscuit was.

We were once again saying thank you for the Howard Hospital being there now for John. At Doc's suggestion, Dad had left the emergency room and then came out to the car to get me, leaving John in the care of the nurses and Doc and Mom. We sat down outside together on the hospital steps, talking. He told me Doc said that John would be OK with a few stitches and some medicine. His eyes were OK, as the wound had missed them.

Then Dad and I discussed what we would do with my dog, Laddie. The little black and white Cocker Spaniel had been my constant companion since the Stempels gave him to me as a pup at their Willowbrook Ranch. He followed me around in a very protective way, and watched out for me. He went with me and my horse on long rides across the Sherwood and the Ridgewood hills. At Sherwood, he knew exactly, to the minute, when I was due to appear walking back down the road from school, and he waited for me on a particular spot at the bottom of the driveway near the main road. He knew never go out onto the main road.

Doc Babcock in WW I, where he served as a doctor

Doctor Raymond Babcock

If I happened to be later than usual because I had stopped to play a game or two of hopscotch in the soft road dust in front of the James house, or to pick wildflowers to bring home, his face would get longer and longer as he waited. When I appeared at the top of the last rise in the road, he would be so happy to see me that he would jump up and stand dancing and wiggling all over on his one special spot at the bottom of the driveway. When I got to him, he would greet me with enthusiastic affection. As soon as I started up the driveway, he would cut loose and run in his "happy dog circles" up the road ahead of me and all across the barnyard up to our house. Then he would stand on the front stairs wagging his tail until Mom knew I was home, like he was the one delivering me safely there.

All this made it a very difficult and tearful time for us, knowing what a dear dog Laddie was, and knowing what had just happened with my little brother. We talked about how it happened, what had happened, and if it was likely to happen again. I was in the same room with John and Laddie, but I hadn't seen exactly how it happened. All I knew was that my brother and the dog were at my feet while I was lying on my bed reading. My Mom was adamant about getting rid of the dog, my Dad was trying to see all sides, and I was trying to be fair, bracing myself against losing my dog, and knowing that he had hurt my brother badly, intentionally or not.

After Doc Babcock had properly stitched up John's nose and cheek, and we saw that it was not as bad as it had looked at first, we were all so relieved. We started the long quiet drive back home to Ridgewood, and there was more time to think. When we arrived back home, we went upstairs and Mom took John in and got him comfortable and into bed. Dad let Laddie out of the closet. The dog knew he had done wrong, and as he crept back into the room, he hung his head low as if offering his apologies. He wouldn't look up at anyone, and he was very, very, downcast. So was I.

After some further family discussion about the whole situation, Dad decided we would keep Laddie, under the condition that the dog and John be kept far apart. It was a deal. The dog always had sore ears, with stickers easily getting caught up in his long, cocker spaniel, curly-haired ears. It was a known problem with that breed. John, at his age, was naturally curious about things, and he may have reached out to pet Laddie's long soft looking curly ears. Whatever had taken place, it all turned out far better than it had looked in the beginning, with the issues being resolved. John healed up fine, and Laddie gave him lots of room, and eventually they became friends again. We had Laddie in our family until we left Willits to move to Pleasanton about four years later.

## BILLY THE KID

While we lived there at the Upper Mare Barn, my Dad, who was somewhat of a horsetrader, bought this fine looking little white and chestnut pinto gelding from a trick rider that had used the horse in her act at Madison Square Garden in New York. He no doubt bought the classy looking little horse for his resale value. On command, without any bridle on him, he would bow, count, nod his head "yes", park, and stand and stay where you told him to while you crawled under his belly, between his back legs, or did anything that might make other horses nervous. He had nice conformation, and a smooth singlefoot way of going, almost like a Peruvian Paso horse does. Some riders found his gait unnerving, but I got along with it quite well. I loved learning how to make him do his "tricks". "Billy The Kid", my trick horse!

He wasn't mine, he was a buy-and-sell horse right then, but we became fast friends anyway. I rode him daily, all day when I could. We found out that he was quite a good cow horse, sometimes nearly unseating me with his sharp turns in the corral when we were working cattle. My Dad even used him as a rope horse. Billy's white hair got all over my jeans because I mostly rode bareback. Didn't bother me, but it sure gave my Mom fits with the laundry! She asked me to please ride with a saddle pad to minimize the white horsehair problem.

I kept this new horse in the corrals right there by the Upper Mare Barn where we lived, and how nice it was to have him so handy. Didn't have to walk across any pasture to catch him up to ride. Billy was sure the nicest for me of all the horses my Dad had bought and sold. I also liked riding him better than any of the ranch horses that I had the use of.

## THE POLO PONY

My Dad brought a big, tall, leggy chestnut polo pony home one time, later on. He said that I could ride him if I could catch him, and get up on him by myself. He also said, emphatically, not to ever let his head out, because he was used to racing around the polo fields, and to always ride this horse with a saddle, and added that it was hard to stop him once he got going ... and don't ever use spurs on him!

I caught the polo pony up one day, got him saddled, and got on. My, he was a tall horse! He carried his head so high, as polo ponies do, that it was hard to keep him in check. I was riding him that afternoon out across the field to a fenceline trail to go see if I could find the deer herd in their usual spot at this time of day. The big horse seemed to relax, so I gave him some reins, to which he responded with a faster gait. Whoops, wrong signal! Very quickly, we were off and running!

I gathered up leather fast, but he was already on a high gallop and had caught me off balance. As I pulled up on the reins, the back of his head came up into my face, and he galloped still faster, in a climbing sort of motion. I pulled, and pulled, but I couldn't feel his mouth. And he kept running faster. The eye-level white fence post tops that we had passed by slowly earlier were now whizzing by faster and faster until they became a white blur. He had a very rough side to side canter, and it was hard for me to stay in the saddle at that increasing speed. I pulled and pulled on the reins and hollered, "Whoa!" repeatedly, but it didn't seem to phase him. It began to seem like he could run like this for ten miles ... I wondered what "Plan B" was!

In the back of my mind I was hoping Dad wouldn't come along and see me letting this horse get out of control. I finally got the horse slowed down, and eventually stopped, more his idea than mine. I still had the reins held tight, and I never put the reins down, or even gave him an inch of slack ever again. He was breathing hard, and sweating some. So was I. In a few minutes, I regained my composure. I smoothed my hair back, re-sat in the saddle, all the time keeping a tight choking hold on the reins with one hand. Then I slowly and carefully turned the horse around, and we headed back up the trail for the barn. I walked him, hoping he would cool out before we got back to the barn. I tried to look casual, even though my pounding heart still sounded as loud as Red's hooves had sounded hitting the ground while he was running away. But now I did have control of the situation again. I decided that I didn't care for his way of going, and probably wouldn't be riding him again. I thought it was a good thing that no one had seen me and witnessed my fiasco with the new polo pony.

That night at dinner, Dad surprised me by saying, quietly but sternly, "I told you to never let that horse's head out. I happened to see you from the house here when I was home for lunch." I knew that from the house he had a full view of the whole activity. No more was ever said about it, and the red polo pony was soon gone to a new owner who had use for such a horse. I didn't miss him.

## BUCKY THE FAWN

One late afternoon, one of the ranch riders came by the corrals near our Upper Mare Barn apartment where I was outside brushing Billy the Kid. He called me over to his horse to see what he had on the saddle with him. It was a little fawn, just a few days old. He had come across it early in the morning on his ride on the way out to check the cattle that day. The fawn was laying all alone in the shade of a little bush, where his mother had left him.

When the rider came back, the little fawn was still in the same spot. He stopped his horse, then dismounted and walked over to get a closer look. A mad mother doe should have come to the scene to protect her baby, but none appeared. The rider could see that the little guy was alone and hungry. It would be getting cold soon, and he would be an easy mark for the predators that night. So the cowboy picked him up, got on his horse, and rode on back down the trail toward home.

The cowboy stopped by The Upper Mare Barn where we lived then, and asked if I would like to take care of the little fawn. He said that I better go ask my folks first if it was OK with them. I raced upstairs to ask them, and Dad and Mom said OK, as long as I would do the feeding and tending to the little guy. What a deal! Of course I would!

I ran back down the stairs and told the cowboy that my folks said "OK"! Then I gathered that little fawn in my arms, and took him to a small corral just below my upstairs bedroom window. We needed to make him a bottle soon, or get him some oats, or something because he was hungry and weak. I made him a little bed in a box with a blanket in it, which he didn't stay in very long. I fed him and petted him, all the while getting a real close look at his pretty white spots and his cute little face with the big brown eyes. He soon came to think of me as his Mama, since I was the one that fed him and looked in on him several times a day.

He ate well, grew and filled out, got taller and we watched him play and buck and try out his legs. He seemed to be quite happy here. The only thing he didn't like was my horse, Billy The Kid, and the feeling was mutual. We knew that one day we would be turning Bucky out to go back to the woods again.

That day came quite unexpectedly! One morning after feeding my horse, I came out with Bucky's can of omalene to feed him. I ducked under the fence, as usual, and into his pen to put feed in his bucket. As I looked up from under the fence, I saw him over me, with hooves flying in my direction. I quickly backed out of the fence and straightened up, talking to him, thinking he was playing. No, he was not playing, he meant business. He had grown up, was a big buck now, and he wanted out. He didn't like the smell of my horse on my clothes, and he was taking charge!

I went and tearfully told my Dad what had happened, and he seemed to understand what we must do next. "It is time to return Bucky to the woods", he said . "You have done

Bucky the Fawn and Jani on a rare outing

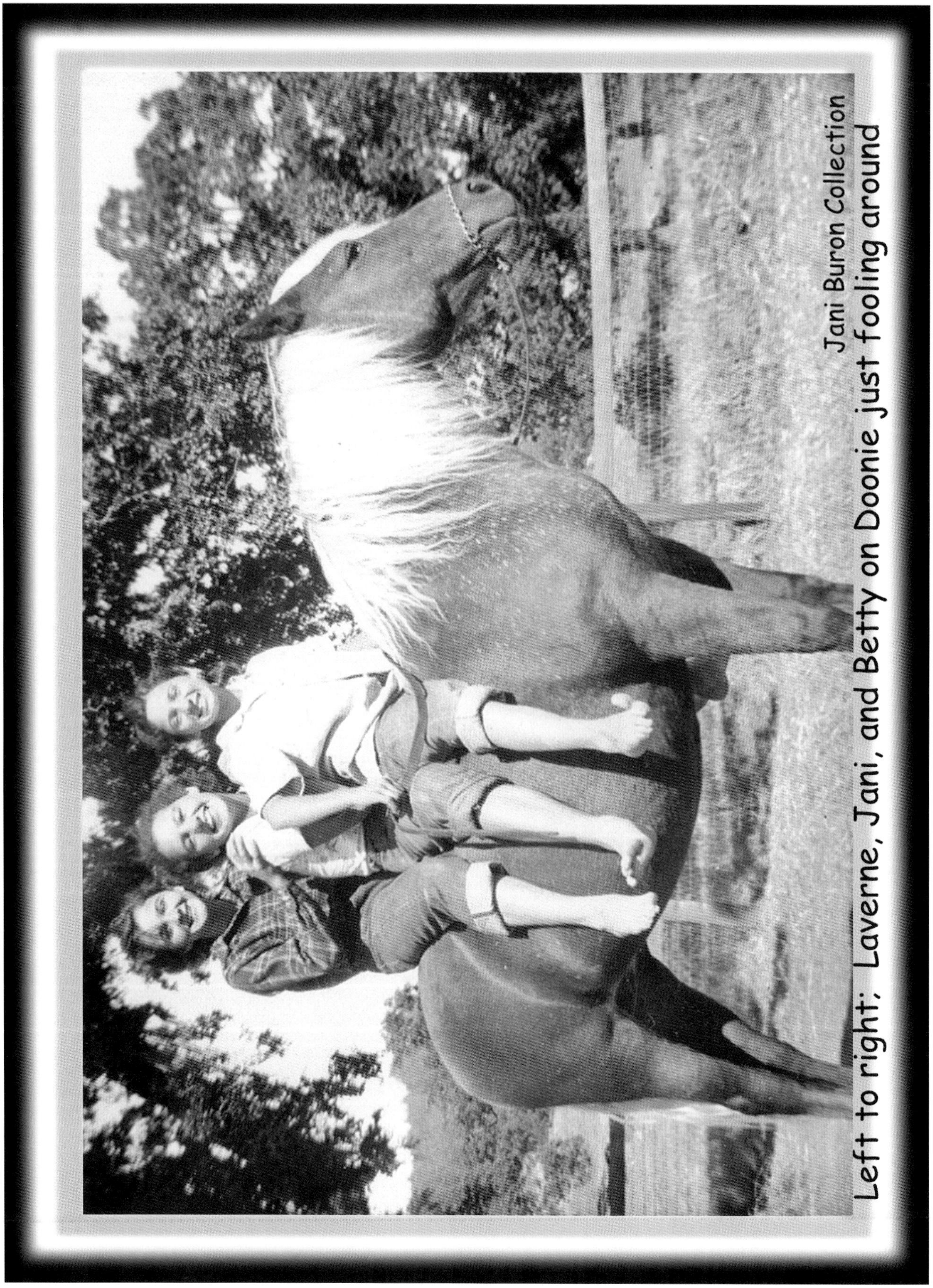

Jani Buron Collection

Left to right: Laverne, Jani, and Betty on Doonie just fooling around

a good job of raising him, and now he is grown up, and ready to go back to his own deer herd. Those flying hooves can hurt you badly, and that is how he is going to be from now on, because he has grown up." Dad got some of the ranch hands to come get him, and take him back to the woods. So I said good-bye to Bucky, and I shall always remember how much fun it was to raise him when he was a little fawn, being so close to a wild animal and learning his ways.

## WE THREE GIRLS

This picture shows us "just being silly". It was one of those days! We took our boots off and rolled our jeans up like the "city kids" did. We put just a halter shank around the nose of Betty's little pumpkin-colored pony named Doonie. Then, one at a time, we all three got on Doonie bareback, which was quite a thing in itself, and we really got the giggles. We were by Seabiscuit's Stud Barn when we did all this, and Sarge saw all the antics. He said we needed a picture of this, so while we posed with funny curled up toes and silly grins, he used my camera and snapped this memory of our happy day!

Jani Buron Collection

The Author Jani Buron on "Billy The Kid" at Ridgewood Ranch in 1948

# Chapter 4

## GROWING UP AT RIDGEWOOD

The new house finally got finished, and it was time to move in. We were ready to be in larger quarters, except for the fact that I enjoyed living so close to the horses, in the same barn even, and having the corrals right there. I would miss that.

Our new house had three bedrooms. One was like a sleeping porch at the far end of the house. It had transom-like windows that opened all the way around the room. Dad liked that one for all the fresh air coming in. The other two bedrooms were at the front end of the house, with an adjoining bathroom between. These bedrooms had walls of combed plywood, very fashionable for the day. The front bedroom was tinted a coral-rose color, the middle one was tinted pale blue. Mom put my brother and me in the blue room, with the one window, leaving the other room with the two windows as a playroom and a guestroom, and for Grandma's visits.

The house had a big service porch at the back door, a moderate sized kitchen, a large living-dining room, and at the front entry to the East, a large sun porch. This glassed-in sun porch that Marcela had built into the house at my Mom's request was great in the wintertime, so warm and comfortable. It was a good place to look out over the hay-pasture meadows to the pear orchard and beyond it, the little stand of Redwoods, and then Lion Mountain. This house was built on the exact same spot the Jones Family's old house had stood. I had lived in that house with them for about a year, so here I was looking out at the same views from a new house that my own family lived in now!

In back of our new house stood a cute little white cottage type house that had been built long ago and maintained very well. When we first moved in, a couple named Rosie and Gene Smith from Nevada lived in the little white house. Later, after they moved away, the Fraser Family lived there. They had two boys named Alan and Cecil, a few years younger than me.

One of the nicest features of where we were now was the fact that I could keep Billy the Kid in the pasture right below the house! That made it so easy to go riding; just grab the bridle, go down the steep sidehill to his pasture, climb over the fence at the bottom, call Billy over and put the bridle on, throw a leg over him bareback, and ride over to the far gate, and go out riding! When I didn't have time to go for a ride, I would go down and climb up the apple tree just inside the fence corner, and he'd come over to see me. I would then drop onto his back from the apple tree limb, and we'd just sit there and visit in the shade. I picked apples off the tree and fed him one now and then. That is why he came over to see me when I went down to his pasture!

This field where I kept Billy had a high wire fence, and one time when Betty, Laverne, and I went down to catch up the horses, we saw three young buck deer running in circles out in the field. They had jumped downhill over the fence into the pasture, and didn't know where to get out again. They got scared when they saw us coming after the horses and felt threatened. In self-defense, they came after us. We thought we could scare them off by standing our ground and swinging the bridles at them. But guess what... that just made them madder! You never saw three girls retreat and scramble so fast up that almost impassable tall horsewire fence!

The special horse wire that Mr Howard used on the ranch is not made to stick your toes in and climb; it is made of small rows of side-by-side triangles, alternately pointed up then down, of very strong wire that you may be able to get four fingers through, but not big enough for the toes of your boots to dig in! What a sight that must have been; three young buck deer chasing three girls over the tall fence, horses running around in several directions, and plenty of hollering back and forth! I don't know how we ever scaled that fence, not being able to get our feet in and really climb. Guess fright gives you that added adrenaline to do what is necessary to get out of danger!

Later, we found that the only way we could get those bucks out of the pasture was to open the far gate, keep the horses back, and show the deer the way out by kind of slowly herding them in that direction until they saw the open gate, and freedom! They were happy to see an opening in the fence. It took several of us to accomplish this. We didn't ever see deer back in that pasture again, so they must have spread the word about their experience to the rest of their family!

## HEN'S NEST

One warm Spring day I finally got home from school after an especially long school bus ride around the valley in Willits. It seemed to me that the bus was really running late, and had more stops than usual. We got to the Forestry Station, then from the Forestry to the Ranch, and I remember being so glad to get home while there was still

Laverne at the lake on a colt "Rosie"

Jani Buron Collection

Jani with Billy The Kid in the pasture next to their new house enough daylight to ride. I hurriedly changed from my school clothes into my jeans and tee shirt, grabbed my bridle, and headed out the door to the shortcut trail down the hill to the pasture.

The steep oak tree shaded sidehill between our house and the pasture below had now dried out some from the Spring rains, and trail had turned from mud to damp ground. The trail had long, lush green grass leaning over it and covering it up, but I knew where the trail was supposed to be. The low hanging oak tree limbs almost touched the ground on the uphill sides of the trees, so steep was the terrain. I took the direct shortcut down the hill, dodging the low tree branches, bounding downhill two or three feet at a time. There was no real trail and the descent was almost like a controlled free fall over the thick green grass.

Suddenly I lost my footing when I unexpectedly stepped on something squashy. I slipped and fell back into a small hollow of ground and heard .... and felt ... a strange crunch. Then I smelled it! A huge nest full of rotten eggs that was long since laid and left there by some old setting hen! In my haste to get down the hill, I had jumped directly in the middle of the nest and then fallen back into it. The odor of rotten eggs that released was a horrible choking combination of all the worst smells I had ever encountered. The nest was so big, especially after I had flattened it out, that the only way to get up was to crawl out of it, getting broken rotten eggs pasted to me on all sides. My prized bridle I had in my hand that I had saved up $14. and sent to Colorado for, had raw egg and broken eggshell stuck all over it.

My horse had come over to the fence, expecting to see me, and suddenly he turned away, with a funny look on his face, his nostrils twitching. I couldn't blame him; I was choking, too. I looked down at myself, and my jeans looked like scrambled eggs and my boots were crusted with the stuff. I slowly started climbing back up the hill; the only way to go back up this steep hill was slow. The odor followed me. We usually used this part of the hill only as a "down" trail, and came up where it was not as steep. As I approached the house, my Mom was outside and heard me coming back early. She walked around the corner of the house to see what was the matter. She got a whiff of me and ran for the garden hose, repeating something about, "Don't go near the house!" She hosed me off, then I discarded my rotten jeans and tee shirt outside the back porch door, and went inside to regroup, still smelling like rotten eggs.

I got my bridle clean first, then bathed and scrubbed myself, until I was once again socially acceptable. The reminiscence of that awful odor stayed with me for a long

A 1940 colt, Sea Convoy by Seabiscuit out of Illeana, 2nd of the 1st seven

time, and I sure stayed clear of that area of the sidehill. I didn't eat any eggs for long time, either!

## LOWER MARE BARN

My Dad's duties at Ridgewood included looking after all of the Howards' Thoroughbred broodmares. Mr. Howard purchased well bred, beautiful mares, and bred them mostly to his own fine stallions. Travel from breeding farm to breeding farm for horses in the 1940s was not as convenient as it is today. The two lane highways were slower going, and during World War II the gas rationing limited travel. So Mr. Howard selected and brought his own fine court of mares to his stallions for his Thoroughbred breeding operations.

The Lower Mare Barn located at the southern end of the main ranch compound, was the foaling barn. It had spacious well-lighted stalls, deep shedrows, nice tack rooms, and lots of paddocks and runs for the mares and foals to exercise in. There was a little office with a desk and a couple of chairs where the men stayed in between doing their rounds of checking the mares in labor. Medical supplies were also kept in here, and a pot of coffee was always going. The chart that kept track of each mare's progress and her foal's date and time of birth was on the desk. During foaling season this was not a visitors barn like the Stud Barn was. This barn was kept quiet and immaculately clean, and you had better ask before you go in there, in the event a mare was foaling and didn't need to be startled by some unexpected noises or strange people.

I went in there at night with Dad while he quietly checked on the mares in labor and those who had just given birth. He talked with the different men that were watching over the barn, and asked if anything else was needed. It was always so wonderful to see the tiny newborns as they tried with such determination to get up on their wobbly legs for the first time. I even got to see a couple of them being born.

After foaling season, people would come at the Howards' invitation to see the mares and new foals out enjoying the sunshine in their paddocks. Charles and Marcela would point out the current crop of "Little Biscuits", sired by their favorite famous horse, Seabiscuit. The visitors speculated and discussed the fine points of each foal, agreed and disagreed on which ones were the best bred ones and which ones would likely run the fastest, and what they were worth. Mr. Howard and Marcela were always so proud to show off the new crop, and accepted the praise of their fine selection of horses gracefully. They really loved their horses, and always provided the best of care and equipment for them.

Jani Buron Collection

An attraction at Ridgewood Ranch, this Appaloosa colt found an eager buyer

One of the most unusual attractions of any foaling season was a little chestnut Thoroughbred foal who had developed a perfect blanket of spots on his rump. He was of definite interest to the world of Appaloosa race horse breeders. Many people came to see him, and commented on the rarity of Thoroughbred breeding with the result being an Appaloosa colt. We heard that several people had offered Mr. Howard large sums of money for him immediately when signs of a blanket began to appear; one figure being talked about was $100,000, which was quite a handsome offer for a horse in that time.

When the foaling season was over, we children were allowed to go in and see the new babies out in their pens anytime during the day. We could watch the patient young men handling the young colts and fillies, walking them along the shedrows of the barn while talking softly to them. They were teaching the young horses to walk beside someone in a straight line, don't bite, and don't kick, and don't fight the rope! The foals started out by wearing a tiny halter attached to a soft cotton rope wrapped around the foal's hindquarters going just below their round little rumps, to help urge them along in a forward motion. At first, the leggy colts usually pranced along with their tiny hooves flying in all directions, and all bug-eyed and with their necks arched in protest. They would sometimes let out an occasional squeal or a high-pitched whinny calling for Mom to come get them. They were ducking and diving to try and get some distance from their handlers. After they learned about walking straight beside someone, they would then walk proudly with just the halter and shank on, looking at their handler, as if to say, "Aren't you proud of me now?" This was all in preparation for learning about getting saddled up and having human weight on their back about the time they were two years old. That would be quite an experience for them!

Frank Tours was one of those young men who handled the foals. He had a genuine love for horses and a strong but gentle hand with them. When my family left Ridgewood in 1950 to go to the Pleasanton Racetrack so Dad could start his racing stable, we saw Frank there, too. Sometimes he worked with my Dad. Frank told us one day that he was going to trade in his blue-jeans for a suit and tie, and go to the Southern California racetracks to accept a job working in the publicity and public relations department. That he did and he was good at it, and became very dedicated to the sport of Thoroughbred racing. He was instrumental in getting the stakes races from Hollywood Park, Santa Anita, and Del Mar on live TV. Frank's knowledge of the operations on the frontside, combined with his experience on the backside, and his understanding of horsemen's needs, along with his journalism and scriptwriting talents, took him to racetracks from coast to coast. He held management positions at Hollywood Park, Santa Anita, Del Mar, Hialeah, Oak Tree, Latonia, (now Turfway Park), New York Racing Association, and the California Fairs. Frank is well remembered for his many contributions to racing.

Terry Tours Collection

Frank in later years; see pg.135

Jones Family Collection

Frank Tours training a Seabiscuit colt to lead

Jones Family Collection

Betty on Doonie, her shirt is a gift from Marcela Howard

Jani Buron Collection

C.S. Howard had this stud barn built primarily for Seabiscuit at Ridgewood

# Chapter 5

## THE STUD BARN, AND SEABISCUIT AT HOME

The Stud Barn at Ridgewood was a world all its own. It was the center of the public part of the Ranch, and yet so connected to every other part, too. It was a well designed structure, standing squarely amid the paddocks and oak trees, welcoming all the visitors who came to see the great Howard horses. Marcela's designing touch was evident from the flowers she added by the front of the barn. On either side of the large sliding double door at the front of the barn was a window with a window box underneath. Those boxes were always brimming with colorful and fragrant flowers in season, mostly red and white petunias. The white flower boxes had small red Triangle "H" painted on the front. The well-known Howard red and white Triangle "H" was painted in the center above the entrance door. The Triangle "H" was used on the racing colors, and the Quarter Circle "H" was used to brand the Ridgewood livestock. The well-groomed flowerbeds on the ground below them displayed even more colorful blooms.

Outside the barn doors in the front, on each side stood a little statue of a jockey wearing the Howard racing silks. Each figurine had an arm extended out with a hitching ring in it where you could tie up a horse. These little jockeys were a big attraction for the children who came to the ranch with their families to visit Seabiscuit. The children were about the same height as the jockeys, and they could identify with them. Many a photo was taken with these little jockeys!

The road that turned off Highway 101 at the famous Redwood arch, with Mr. Howard's proud sign hanging from the top proclaiming "Ridgewood Ranch, Home of Seabiscuit" led straight to the Stud Barn, and did not go through any other part of the ranch headquarters. The travelers had a good view of the oak woodlands of the Ridgewood hills and the lush pastures on either side of the road coming in.

Visitors parked their cars under the cool oak trees in front of the barn while they went inside to see the stallions. It was such a pretty setting that the people usually enjoyed lingering there, taking in the country scenery.

The tall, rugged featured, soft spoken former military man named Sarge greeted all the visitors, and asked them to please do us the honor of signing the great guest book just inside the door. Sarge would also entertain people with stories if they lingered long

Jani Buron Collection

Charles and Marcela Howard at the new Stud Barn at Ridgewood

Jani Buron Collection

Sarge, in charge of the Stud Barn at Ridgewood Ranch

John Bosko Collection

Seabiscuit is in the cameras eye, at the Upper Mare Barn in 1940

enough for him to get started. Sarge's Dalmation dog, Anita, was usually nearby looking proper and dignified as she helped welcome the visitors.

Sitting beside the guest book on the waist high table was a stack of little folders that Mr. Howard had printed so each visitor could have a souvenir from Ridgewood to take home with them. The folder had a black and white picture of Seabiscuit standing by an oak tree on the front, and inside was his pedigree, and a paragraph describing his racing career accomplishments. We children would occasionally take one of the little folders home, and carefully paint watercolor onto Seabiscuit and the green trees, making quite a colorful picture of him!

People from all over the world had been there and signed the guest book; the famous and the ordinary, the horseman and non-horseman, curious tourists, fans of the horseracing world, who returned again and again, and people of all ages, all kinds, from many countries, young and old. Mainly they came to see the champion horse, Seabiscuit, the horse with the great heart who had overcome many hardships to eventually display his amazing speed, determination, intelligence, and the ability to come back even after adversity struck. He had the heart and soul of a champion, and people loved him for it.

Sarge would usher the visitors into the barn where they walked across the red cork-brick floor and past the four large stalls, one in each corner, usually telling an interesting story about one horse or another as he went. Then he took them out to the paddock area to see the Howard stallions, the most famous being Seabiscuit. Ironically, he was the most ordinary looking. The other studs liked to show off by prancing around their paddock with their tail held high, shaking their head, getting the attention of the crowd. But The Biscuit would just continue whatever he was doing, eating or sleeping under the oak tree, or standing all relaxed in the shade, almost asleep on his feet. He was a past master at the art of napping. He would sometimes look in the direction of the voices calling to him, "Hi Seabiscuit!", and on rare occasion, he might even stroll over to the fence for a few minutes, to be sociable, looking his visitors over one by one. Then he would saunter back to his favorite corner and resume the fine art of relaxing. The visitors would sometimes stay for a long time on the little viewing platform that Mr. Howard had provided for them, and gaze at Seabiscuit while they recalled his memorable races. The little horse from the West, with the big heart, who had beat noble and larger horses from coast to coast had endeared himself to America forever.

By the time Seabiscuit came to Ridgewood to retire from racing, he was seven years old. His bay color became darker, and he loved to just enjoy life, taking it easy and doing lots of eating and sleeping. He had raced often and hard, and had come back from

John Bosko Collection

Seabiscuit in front of the Stud Barn at Ridgewood for a photo shoot

injuries that would have sidelined any lesser horse. He had a glorious racing career, and still had a loving public. He enjoyed rolling in the soft dirt of his paddock, which is a cleansing and cooling act for a horse. He especially liked doing this right after his bath, to the exasperation of the grooms who had a hard time keeping him clean of dust and presentable for his public. Seabiscuit was a free spirit, and he did whatever he thought was right to do at the time. Usually it was right for him, and was accepted by everyone!

The many tourists who came there to see him used to exclaim over this wonder horse, and talk about his racing accomplishments, and refer to events that all started happening before I was born! Some of the visitors asked us if this ordinary looking horse was really The Biscuit! Of course he was; he was in that same paddock when I first came to Ridgewood! That was his home.

Seabiscuit was very aware and interested in other animals and their activities. He liked most of them. One Mama kitty insisted on always having her kittens in the deep straw of Seabiscuit's stall. He would allow her room, and before he lay down for a nap, he was careful to look around and see where she and her kittens were nested. After The Biscuit passed on, and her time was getting near again, the Mama kitty looked around and went in and out of the other horses stalls to find a suitable place to have her babies. She was not happy with any of them. She finally was satisfied to go back into Sea Sovereign's stall to give birth to her new family. Sea Sovereign looked more like Seabiscuit than any of his other offspring.

Movie stars often came to see Seabiscuit, and to visit with the Howards. Some enjoyed going to the races, or just coming to see Ridgewood, and others had their own racing stables and were interested in the Thoroughbred mares and studs on the Ranch. Seeing some of the Hollywood set there was a common sight for us, and they were there to see the horses, and we never thought it important or interesting to ask them for autographs. Bing Crosby was a regular guest of the Howards. Clark Gable and friends and George Brendt all visited, too, among other notable Hollywood personalities.

## SEABISCUIT'S FIRST FOALS

In 1939 when Seabiscuit came to Ridgewood to heal up from his racing injuries, he was also bred to seven of Mr. Howard's top Thoroughbred mares. His first crop was born in 1940, and there was much celebration and grand speculation of the champion's offspring. Pictures of the "Little Biscuits" with their sire's photo in the center were designed into a Christmas card that became a favorite with Seabiscuit fans. The list of the first crop of foals follows.

John Bosko Collection

Seabiscuit and Mr. Howard were real buddies, both enjoyed their time together

**Sea Belle**, b. f. by Seabiscuit out of Flying Belle, by Flying Ebony.
**Sea Convoy**, ch c. by Seabiscuit out of Illeanna, by *Polynesian
**Sea Frolic**, b. f. by Seabiscuit out of Sun Frolic, by *Sun Briar.
**Sea Knight,** b.c. by Seabiscuit out of Fair Knightess, by Bright Knight
**Sea Mite,** ch. f. by Seabiscuit out of Dressage, by *Bull Dog
**Sea Patrol**, br. c. by Seabiscuit out of Lady Riaf, by *War Cry.
**Sea Skipper,** b. c. by Seabiscuit out of Lucille K., by Whiskalong
* Imported horses

## SEABISCUIT AND THE BRIDGE

Mr. Howard rode Seabiscuit around the Ranch, and I often wondered how such a great race horse could also be such a nice saddle horse, since most of the horses I had seen from the track were really excitable. By contrast, Kayak II, Ajax, Sabu, Mioland and the others would show off for the visitors, prancing and rearing and putting on a show.

Mr. Howard and Seabiscuit really had a friendship going; each liked and trusted the other. I heard a story retold several times about a ride Mr. Howard took on Seabiscuit during the Spring floods, a high-water time for all the creeks and rivers there in the Walker Valley. They rode down through the ranch headquarters and started up the road toward The Lake. When they got to the bridge on that road, with the high water rushing under it, Seabiscuit refused to put a foot onto that bridge. Mr. Howard wanted to cross, so he urged him again and again to walk on it. The sturdy little horse continually refused, and a short time later, that bridge was washed off its foundation by the rushing floodwaters. Seabiscuit knew that bridge was unsafe, and saved himself and Mr. Howard from great danger.

## SEABISCUIT IS GONE, ONLY HIS BRONZE STATUE LOOKS ON

Early on the morning of May 17, 1947, while we were eating breakfast, a knock came at the door. My Mom went to answer it, and I could tell by the timbre of the man's voice when he was speaking that something sad had happened. He brought us the news that Seabiscuit had died during the night. He had a heart attack, and nothing could be done to save him. The old horse had passed on peacefully. But he wasn't really an "old" horse, he was only 14! What an empty place he would leave at that Stud Barn! He was one of a kind, a champion's champion, and everyone loved him. Especially Charles and Marcela Howard.

Seabiscuit working at Del Mar 1938, Joe Ferguson up

Marcela and Mr. Howard were devastated by the unexpected and sudden loss of their famous champion horse and companion. Sadness filled the air around Ridgewood. We would not see Mr. Howard riding Seabiscuit around the ranch again. We would not see The Biscuit again napping under his favorite oak tree, or gazing off into the distance in quiet thought, or gently nuzzling one of the barn kitties to say "hello". We would not be able to give him treats of carrots or apples. Seabiscuit was gone, and there would never be another like him.

Now a peaceful resting site suitable for a champion of his stature needed to be selected. That done, the solemn ceremony took place on the same day of his passing. Mr. Howard was there, Curley Jones and his daughter Laverne, the ranch veterinarian, Doc Britton, and the stableman, and a couple of ranch hands to help with the burial. Laverne heard a distraught Charles Howard say, with much emotion, "Seabiscuit will show them how to run in Horse Heaven!" Betty and I were at the site the next day to pay our respects. Of all the people who were in attendance at that time, the only ones still living are Laverne, Betty and I ( Jani ).

Seabiscuit's likeness was displayed so well in his statue at the Santa Anita Park, and it seemed quite a suitable tribute to him. Mr. Howard also had a duplicate statue placed later at Ridgewood near the Stud Barn. The artist, Tex Wheeler, had created the statue in a barn at Ridgewood a few years earlier. Seabiscuit had been led in to view his likeness. He reacted rather casually as he sniffed the nose of his duplicate plaster creation, and must have wondered why the other "horse" hadn't sniffed back to say hello! A lot of locals came to observe Tex Wheeler at work, and offered help if anything was needed. Doc Babcock took home movies of the process from time to time, with the camera that Mr. Howard had given him. Doc took a lot of movie footage all during the Seabiscuit era, at the Ranch and at the racetrack, and we are able to enjoy it today. His foresight in recording this important history is very much appreciated by the current generation of Seabiscuit racing fans and racing history buffs.

We three girls would go look at the statue up close, and look at the fine hairs and the hooves, and the other details that had been so carefully done. It looked so real, just like The Biscuit was standing there gazing off into the distance. Perhaps he was listening to "The Call to the Post". We were asked not to climb on the statue, and to always treat it with respect, which we did.

Very soon, colorful flowers were planted around the base of the statue, and then shrubbery, and then a little circular walkway for guests to walk around it and visit. The

Jani Buron Collection

Seabiscuit statue at Ridgewood Ranch, superbly crafted by Tex Wheeler

little garden was always well groomed, and the flowers bloomed in the Spring, Summer, and the Fall. Mr. Howard had these words carved into the base of the statue:

> *"Biscuit's courage, honesty, and physical prowess definitely placed him among the Thoroughbred immortals of turf history. He had intelligence and understanding almost spiritual in quality."*

We immediately set out to memorize these pretty words, so we could recite them anytime, anywhere. Laverne was the first to successfully memorize the whole thing. Betty and I eventually got it down pat, too.

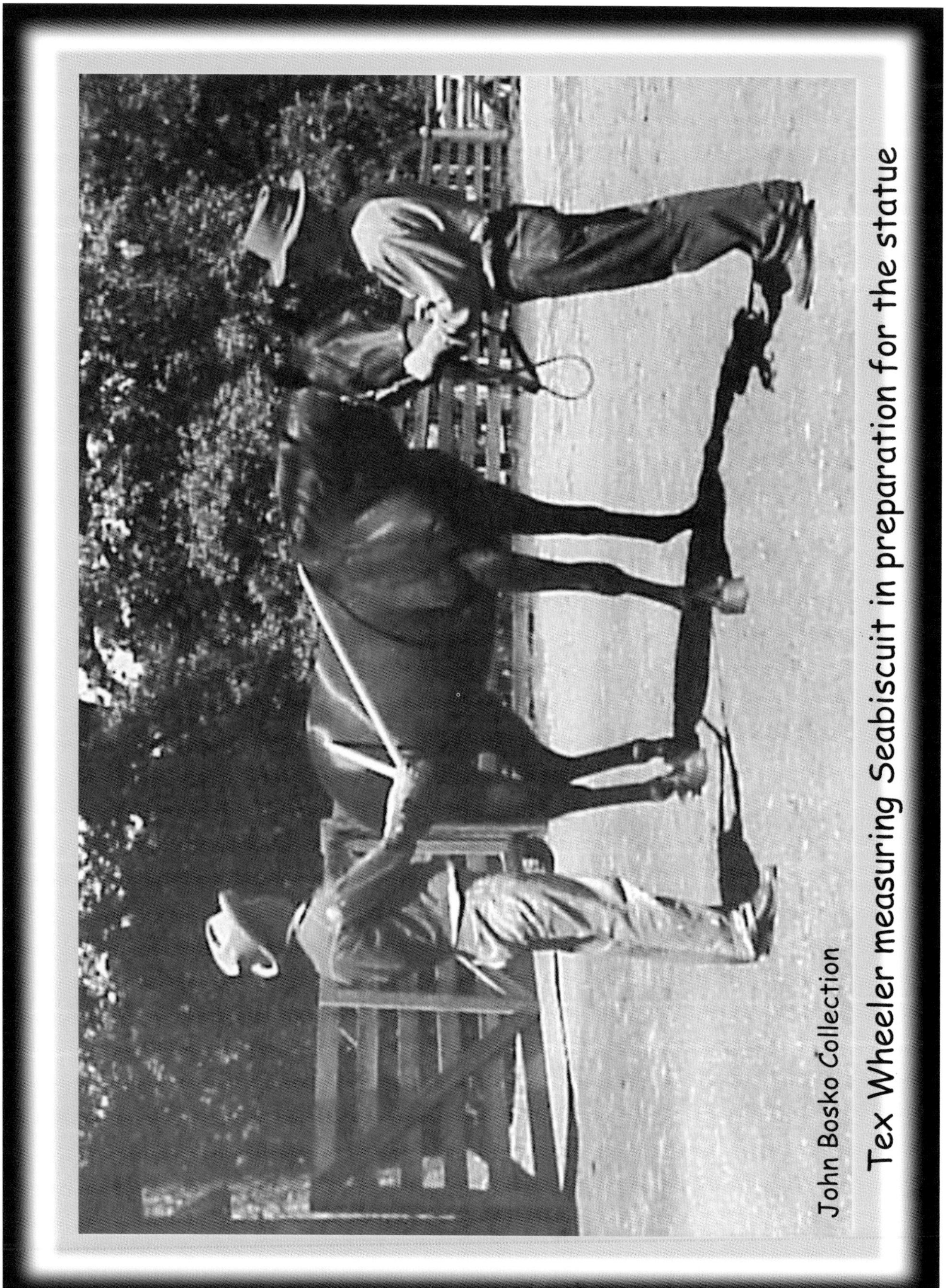

John Bosko Collection

Tex Wheeler measuring Seabiscuit in preparation for the statue

Peggy Ferguson Collection

Seabiscuit at Del Mar, 1938 work during a race day with Joe Ferguson up

John Bosko Collection

Mr. Howard rode Chulo around the ranch. Chulo was his favorite parade horse

# Chapter 6

## THE RIDGEWOOD COMMUNITY

When Mr. Van Arsdale had owned the land that was now Ridgewood Ranch, he had built a new large enclosed reservoir up above the highway that was adequate to serve the needs of the whole Ranch. He piped water down to the ranch and installed a Pelton Wheel in the Power House to generate electricity for the needs of the ranch. The trail from the Ranch to the reservoir went through a tunnel under the 101 Highway, which was quite unique. We thought it was very special to go through that tunnel on horseback while cars drove over us on Highway 101 up on top! Riders from the Ranch went up to check on the reservoir quite often; it was a regular requirement. When we rode that way, we checked on it, too, and reported anything out of the ordinary.

C. S. Howard was at one time considered to be the richest man in America. The newspapers said this, and so did the business world. We children were never aware of his immense wealth, and if someone had asked us about him, we would probably have described him as a kind man who did nice things for people wherever he could. We would have said Marcela was a pretty lady who was very friendly to us, and she also did nice things for people. Together, they were very generous, but we did not realize then that their good deeds took lots of money.

My Mom must have been aware of Mr. Howard's status of wealth. One time as we came back from town through the Ridgewood gate on the highway, we went around the bend, we saw Mr. Howard out riding on Chulo. They were up on the little hill just above the road. As Mom made a turn in the road, the horn on our Chevy malfunctioned, and began to go toot-toot-toot, then it blew constantly, then went back to toot-toot-toot. It stuck like that, as we drove past Mr. Howard! He waved, and then waved again as our horn kept blowing, and then looked after us, wondering, as we continued on down the road going beep-beep-beep! Mom was embarrassed to say the least. We drove on into the main ranch and over to the maintenance shop where one of the mechanics quickly came to our rescue and got the horn stopped.

### SCHOOL BUS AND THE HOWARD FORESTRY

The only reason to go in to town was if you needed some hardware, or a tractor part that couldn't be found on the place, or some specialty item. We Ridgewood kids went to town to attend school. Every weekday morning while school was on, a Chevy panel truck from the ranch came by each family's house to pick us up for school, along with any list for town that our folks might have. The driver took us up the long grade to Willits, dropped us off at our respective schools, then did the town errands, including picking up the Ranch mail and newspapers, and then returned to Ridgewood to deliver the goods.

The school buses would not travel on Ridgewood Grade, up or down. After school we waited 45 minutes for the "second bus", then went out around the East Valley dropping kids off, then to the Howard Forestry Station south of Willits. Mr. Howard had donated the land to build the Forestry station on, so it carried his name. We Ridgewood kids got off the bus there and waited for someone from the ranch to pick us up. Usually our Moms would take turns driving up the grade to get us. My Grandfather, J. C. Philbrick, was the Mendocino County Forestry Superintendent then, and I would get to see him sometimes while we were waiting there after school at the Forestry.

If we had a little wait for our ride home, we would make up games to pass the time. Sometimes we girls amused ourselves by seeing who could run and then jump up to touch the highest rock we could reach on this great slanted stone retainer wall that the Forestry crew had built. It was quite a game, and was certainly more fun than doing homework assignments while we waited for our ride home.

This large slanted wall in the Forestry yard was composed of rows and rows of large flat rocks placed side by side going up and all the way around the end of that hill, from the edge of the road pavement up to the top of the hill. So the challenge to touch the highest rock was endless. The wall was a work of art, each flat stone being placed carefully equidistant from the other, and then skillfully grouted in between. It was built to retain the upper level area of the hill above the main entrance to the Forestry. The employee houses were then built up on that hill under the grove of pine trees. Now the "new" portion of Highway #101 goes around what used to be the backside of the Forestry, and so the stone wall is no longer visible from the main road.

## THE BIG HOUSE - THE BARN - RIDING THE STAGECOACH,

What we called "The Big House", Charles and Marcela Howard's home, stood in a grove of gardens and trees on a hill above the main ranch headquarters. Their private carriage house type saddle horse barn was there, too, and the house was in close proximity to Seabiscuit's quarters in the Stud Barn, although no public road led from one to the other.

The house was a large, quietly elegant, rambling building with dark wood siding. It was built by the previous owners, and designed in a kind of horseshoe shape around a stone patio with a huge outdoor fireplace in it. Several of the rooms opened onto the patio. All kinds of pretty and exotic flowers and shrubbery surrounded the house, and it was all very well tended to by "Norman the English Gardener". Marcela loved her flowers, and saw to it that they were shared with everyone. Whenever Norman had an excess of cut flowers, he brought them down to "Charlie the Vegetable Gardener". Charlie then put bouquets into each family's vegetable box that was left on the big cool cement creamery porch to receive fresh produce. It was always a nice surprise to go pick up your box of fresh vegetables and find lovely fresh-cut flowers in it, too!

Two fulltime maids lived in and looked after the Howard house. I think one of them was called Greta. We thought they were "old maids" , because they were maids, and to us they were old. Wrinkled even. When we knocked on the house door, it took a long time for them to answer it. They had strong foreign accents, and on the few occasions when we did talk to them, we couldn't understand them and they couldn't understand us. All meaningful conversation was lost.

We knew that the kids in town went trick-or-treating on Halloween in their neighborhoods. Since we lived out on a Ranch, there weren't many houses close together for us to carry out this Halloween tradition. However, on one Halloween, one of us got the idea that we should trick-or-treat the maids at the Howard house. That idea turned into a dare, and we soon lost track of exactly who was daring who to do what.

That Halloween evening, after much planning, and under the cover of darkness, we walked up the hill to the Big House, and hid in the garden by the back door. We took turns for several minutes whispering at each other, "You go first!" "No, you go first, then I'll go!" "Who's idea was this, anyway?" Finally someone got brave enough to step out of the bushes and into the yard where the porch light shone, and then knock on the door. When one maid finally opened the door, we all three shouted our best "trick or treat!" yell. Well, she didn't understand what we meant, and we couldn't explain it to her, and when the second maid came to the door, she didn't know either, so the whole thing was a bust. But anyway, someone had gotten brave enough to knock on the door at the Big House on Halloween night! If the Howards had been there at the time, they would have understood what the game was, and enjoyed it. I wish we could have explained to the maids, who were probably very nice ladies.

The Howards' large old saddlehorse barn stood at the top of the driveway, just across the yard from the house. All kinds of treasures were in there; the Howards'

Robert Lee Collection

This Stagecoach was kept in Howard's personal barn and used in parades

ranch saddles, their beautiful silver mounted parade saddles, and silver decorated bridles, and lots of fine tack. That old barn burned down one weekend when the Howards were not there, and some other family members and guests were staying at the Big House. The new barn they rebuilt in its place was large and impressive looking, but somehow did not have the same traditional character as the old barn.

We did go into the new barn to investigate. We entered through a little door on the backside of the barn, always making sure it was closed after us. There was a real stagecoach in there, an old one. Sometimes it was taken into Willits for the Fourth of July Parade as a part of the Ridgewood Ranch parade entry. That coach was the draw for us kids. We would go into the barn quietly, and with all due respect, enjoyed looking at the pretty saddles. Then we would climb up into that coach. We three made it rock and sway, and away we'd go! We made believe that we were travelling across the plains at top speed, side curtains flapping! We took turns being inside the coach, or on top of it in the driver's seat, hee-hawing at the imaginary horses to go faster. I'm not sure we had permission to go in there, but no one actually told us "no", and besides, who could stay away from that magnificent old stagecoach? It made us feel like we were in the Western movies having great adventures!

## THE WHITE DEER OF RIDGEWOOD

The Howards invited many people to come and spend time at their lovely ranch. Among them was William Randolph Hearst. He later sent a gift for the Howards to Ridgewood of 51 White Deer that were imported from India. Their arrival in 1949 created quite a stir. The White Deer were highly revered where they originated in the Mediterranean region, and thought to have a religious connection, and some thought they brought good luck. They were a fine gift.

When the deer were brought to Ridgewood, they were kept in a long, narrow fenced pasture by the Howards' private saddle horse barn. The pasture went down from The Big House through a little draw, and back up toward the Upper Mare Barn. This gave them plenty of room to move around and get acclimated to their new environment, while at the same time being observed by the veterinarians and ranch workers who checked regularly on their well-being. We checked on their well-being, too, and satisfied our curiosity about what a white deer was. An animal from far-off India, yet! We would go quietly up to the fence and watch these strange creatures. They looked like a cross breed of goats and deer, and they seemed to feel foreign in their new surroundings. They looked unsure and shy of the new people and other animals they saw in their new home.

The white deer at Ridgewood are from India and were a gift to Mr. Howard

Those white deer created a new topic for conversation with the press and among the locals. They all came to see the "white deer", some saying they looked more like goats and less like deer. The poor things were so rattled and tired from their long journey that it took a whole month to recover and look like themselves again. We heard that one died due to a shipping mishap, and one died soon after of something else. Once they were here, they received the best of attention and care. When Mr. Howard said the time was right, the deer were turned loose to make their home in the oak tree hills of Ridgewood.

Forty-nine of those white creatures survived to be turned out. They stayed right around the Ranch for awhile, not quite knowing where to go from there. Eventually they began to drift out further and explore the land. They must have eventually felt at home, because they ate well, and looked healthy, and they did proliferate.

They stuck together in one herd for a long time, not mingling with any other native animals. They reproduced, got healthy, learned to live in the Northern California hills and became a self-sustaining group of animals. Later on, due to the color change and conformation we observed in the fawns, we concluded that they had crossbred with the local deer. We didn't know then that the white deer fawns are a light creamy tan color at birth. That provided a lot of fodder for local argument, one side saying they wouldn't cross-breed, and the other side insisting that they already had! Mr. Howard must have been proud of the final outcome, having a healthy herd of White Deer become established there in the Walker Valley; several generations later they probably felt like natives! There are still healthy herds of the white deer at Ridgewood and the surrounding areas and they are seen by the local population on a regular basis.

## THE POOL and THE ORCHARDS

The Big House was completely hidden from view by the lovely shrubbery and gardens surrounding it as well as all the buildings on the hill near it. Marcela loved to have a varied display of unusual and exotic flowers and shrubs everywhere. Amid the gardens near their house, Mr. Howard had an Olympic-size private swimming pool built. An elegantly designed "his and hers" bath house was along one side, and a large lawn on the other. There was a standard low diving board at the deep end, and a two level high dive next to it. A water slide was located at the deep end of the pool in a corner near the diving boards. A shallow wooden wading pool was built right into the main pool at the opposite end. All were first class accommodations. Marcela invited us to swim there whenever they or their guests were not using it. It was a beautiful pool, and we sure made good use of it in the Summertime. I thought that with a pool like that, and if I could get a royal blue swimming suit like I saw Esther Williams wearing in the movies,

The bath house by the Howard home at Ridgewood Ranch

Robert Lee Collection

then surely I could swim like she could! Anyway, I had two out of three, the pool and the suit; my swimming ability never quite equaled Esther Williams, but I sure had fun trying! We still sometimes swam in the creek when we were out riding, but having the use of that pool was the greatest. The Howards were very generous and thoughtful people, as evidenced by their good deeds throughout their lifetime, and by their manner of sharing all they had with family and friends and the community.

One time on an especially hot summer day, we girls decided it would be more fun to go swimming in the Howard pool than to go riding. We changed into our swimming suits at home, then grabbed our bathtowels over our shoulders and started walking up the hill past the orchard to The Big House. It was very hot that day. When we neared the pool we were really ready to jump in, but we saw that several adults were already in it. So, we turned back to go home just as one of them called out to us, "Did you girls come up to go swimming?" We said yes, but we'd come back another day, we didn't know the Howards had company there. They said come on in and cool off now, there was plenty of room. We hesitated, but they insisted, saying they were getting ready to get out and go in the house anyway. So, we gratefully obliged, and got into the cool waters with those other people. Those smiling people having such a good time and including us had very familiar faces, but we weren't sure who they were then. They were just more of the Howards' friends from Hollywood. I do remember a couple of handsome dark haired gentlemen with mustaches and twinkley eyes and big smiles. I guess we could put names on them now! Clark Gable? Douglas Fairbanks Jr.?

Mr. Howard took such pride in his special orchard that produced native and exotic fruits. They were big, productive trees, each one selected for a special reason. That fenced orchard near his house was kept plowed and clean, always. We used to ride up on our horses, coming in from the bottom side through the small gate. We could pick the delicious ripe fruit from the backs of our horses, and even give them an apple or two for getting under the tree just right. ("Billy, move over this way a little so I can reach that big red apple!") What a treat that was. We were asked to pick only what fruit we could eat at the time, because the Howards always enjoyed having some there for the family and guests when they came up. Mr. Howard would proudly walk them through the orchard, telling them how he obtained each special tree.

## MAIN RANCH HEADQUARTERS

The main ranch headquarters was like a little village. The ranch foreman's home was a long low house set under the trees. Originally that house was built for one of the Howard sons and his family. It was near the powerhouse, and another duplex-type house

The Howard Home at Ridgewood Ranch in the 1920's

for ranch families. In the time that we were living on the ranch, three different families occupied the foreman's house; the Briars, the Brittons, and the Morgans.

Within the powerhouse was the ice house, and the freezer room. The freezer room was always well stocked with packages of a variety of Ridgewood-fed meat for the ranch families to choose from. Other buildings located in the main compound were the cookhouse that was attached to a two-story house, one of the oldest buildings on the Ranch, the vegetable gardener's cabin right at the edge of the big garden, the bunk house, a machine shop, a painter's quarters, a slaughter house, a full blacksmith shop, an equipment garage, a saddle horse barn, The Lower Mare Barn, and pens for the hogs, chickens, turkeys, sheep, and pastures for the cows. The place was complete and self-sustaining.

Ridgewood Ranch supplied all the needs for anyone working on the ranch, and some of the meats, the garden produce, and cut flowers also went to the Frank R. Howard Memorial Hospital in Willits. This hospital was generously funded by Mr. Howard, designed by Doc Babcock, and built as a tribute to Mr. Howard's son, Frankie, who lost his life in a single-car accident on Ridgewood in the Spring of 1926. They had felt that if the proper medical facilities had been available, perhaps Frankie could have lived. The hospital, a whole community effort, was completed in 1928. It had the most modern medical equipment available for the day. That hospital served many of us well then, and continues to be an important part of Willits and the surrounding population today.

## THE DAIRY BARN

The dairy barn was a grand one, and supported quite a herd of handsome dairy cows. The white barn stood tall and proud within the ranch headquarters. The crews milked by hand for years, and then came the modern milking machines. Mr. Howard always wanted to keep up with the best and newest systems available, so he ordered a barnful of new milking machines! The dairy hands resisted the change, but there it was in front of them. There was a lot of grousing about all that equipment to clean, and of course some of the cows did not take kindly to the process of getting hooked up to the new contraption. But eventually the cows and the milkers got used to the new method of milking by machine, and all went smoothly again at the Dairy Barn. The milk produced there was top quality, and always had lots of cream on top. It was taken over to the creamery next to the cookhouse where it was put into the hand-turned milk separator. Butter was made from the rich cream. There was always a plentiful supply of dairy products for all the families on Ridgewood.

## THE POWERHOUSE

The powerhouse had large generators in it. We also called it "The Light Plant", referring to the supply of electric lighting to every house and barn and equipment shed on the place. We children never went in there by ourselves. It was an awesome place, with the regular rhythmic sound of the loud diesel generator motor going, and knowing that it supplied electricity to everything on the ranch. This was also the "ice house" where blocks of ice were available, and it was the place we went to pick up our meat. We could choose from fine beefsteaks or hamburger, or chicken, pork, or lamb, all raised on Ridgewood.

## THE SLAUGHTERHOUSE

The livestock that was processed to supply meat for the ranch families was butchered at a facility just beyond the dairy barn. The slaughterhouse and adjoining corrals were very well arranged for convenience and cleanliness. After the animal carcasses were skinned and cleaned, they were hung in the cool room to age properly. The slaughterhouse itself was shaded by large oak trees, so it stayed cool even in the warm weather. We girls were asked to go observe the whole process a couple of times, just as a matter of ranching education. Laverne and Betty's Dad was in charge of that operation.

During the fall deer season, the deer taken on the ranch were cleaned and cut up here too. I recall everyone going to see an especially large buck one year that one of the ranch hands brought in. This buck had a kind of blue cast to his hair. He was the biggest deer I had ever seen up to then. The ranch riders rode the perimeters of the ranch all during deer season to keep out any hunters who were not invited to hunt on Ridgewood. The place was so big that someone might make a mistake and not know that they had drifted onto Ridgewood land. The first time they met up with a line rider, they were given the benefit of the doubt. The second time was a little different.

## THE NIGHT WATCHMAN

A night watchman was always on duty, as a fixture on the ranch. Mr. Howard wanted security for the ranch and its occupants at all times. The watchman had a time clock to punch on the corner of certain barns and buildings during the night. At first, he traveled around inspecting the premises on foot. Later on he drove a little pickup out to each destination, keeping a watchful eye for anything out of the ordinary. He watched

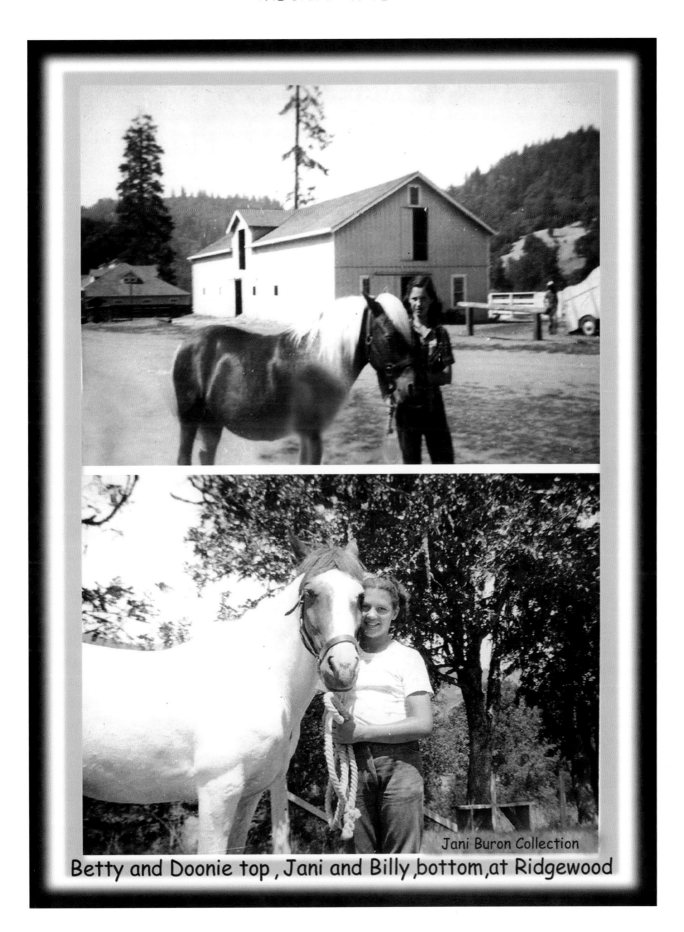

Jani Buron Collection

Betty and Doonie top , Jani and Billy ,bottom,at Ridgewood

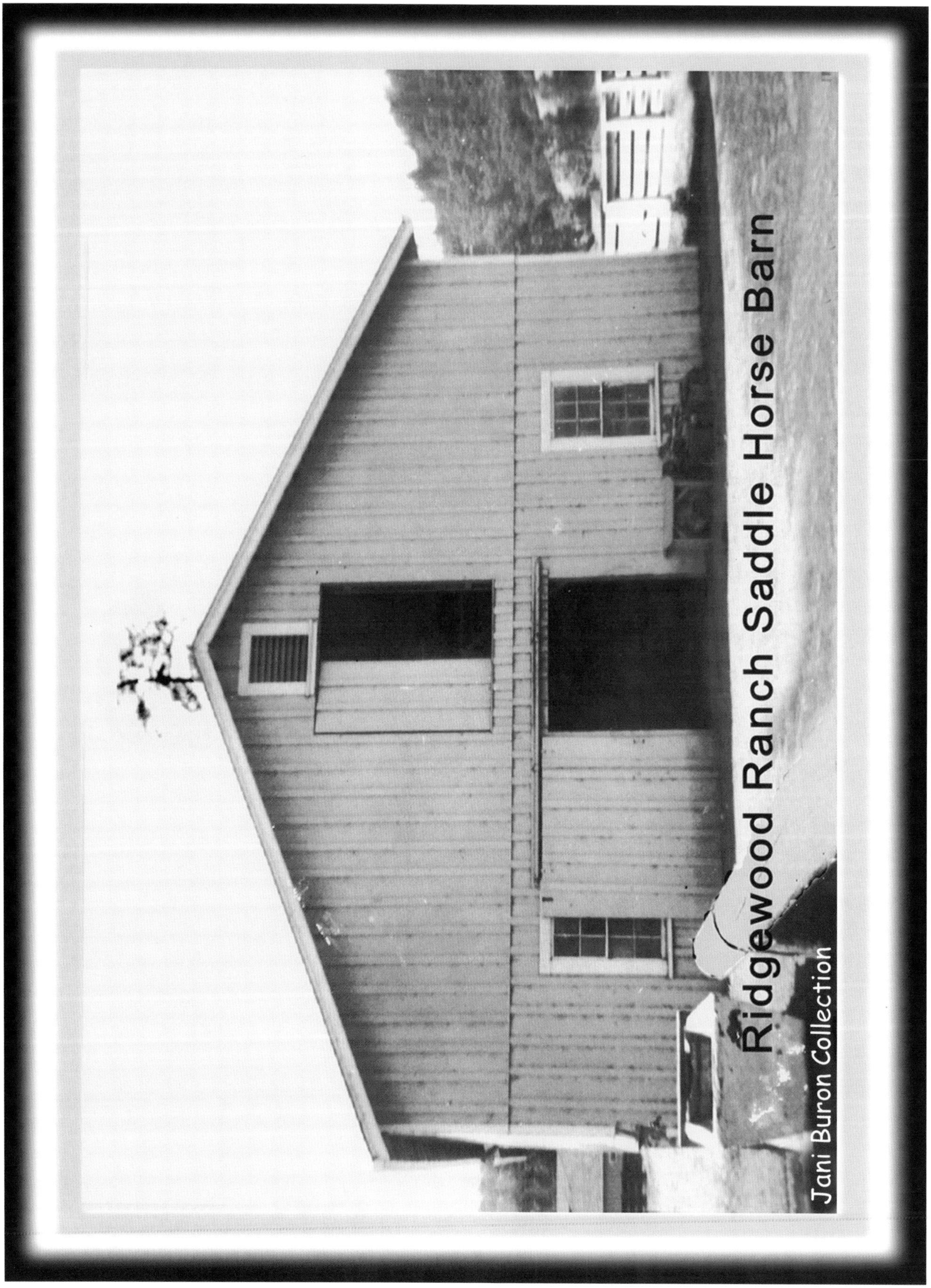
Ridgewood Ranch Saddle Horse Barn
Jani Buron Collection

for intruders, signs of a fire beginning, loose animals, or anything else unusual. We didn't see much of him in the daytime.

## THE SADDLE HORSE BARN

The Saddle Horse Barn was located near the center of the ranch headquarters. The saddle horses were there for the use of anyone on the ranch, as long as you took good care of the horse you used. The supply of horses was rotated between the ranch and the racetrack.

A well supplied tack room was inside the front end of the Saddle Horse Barn. It contained various kinds and sizes of saddles, bridles, halters, and other riding equipment, all neatly kept on racks and hanging hooks. In a little closet under the stairs were all the horse grooming tools needed. A supply of brooms to keep the floor clean stood in the corner.

Outside the front of the barn near the long hitching rail stood a large old handmade cement water trough. It had a big hand-carved wooden plug in one end that took some pounding to get it out to drain the trough. It was our job, we three girls, to keep it clean, since we used the horses more often than anyone else. The cement was aged and worn in many places and moss gathered on the inside where the rough patches were. It took a good scrubbing with a stiff brush to get it clean enough to suit the inspector, ( any adult who looked it over good) so we could refill it. It was a messy job, and it needed more attention in the summertime than in the winter. However, there was a certain satisfaction seeing it refilled with clean clear water after we had washed it out.

We also fed the saddle horses, and sometimes cleaned their stalls. Most of the time they were kept outside in the paddocks. It was easy to feed them from the hay loft; we just pushed a flake of hay across the floor and dropped it into the manger of the stall below. The hayloft always felt cozy and warm, and smelled so good of fresh hay.

## OTHER HEADQUARTERS BUILDINGS

The long narrow series of buildings near the center of the barnyard housed the blacksmith shop, the painting supplies (all the buildings on the ranch were kept clean and painted), the farm machinery, and more. The blacksmith shop was large, and in constant use daily.

The cook house was a single story building attached to the two-story foreman's house. Both had separate entrances, and there was an inside adjoining door between the two residences that was usually kept locked. In the common wall between, there was also a large wide pass-through serving window above a buffet where food could be supplied from the cook's kitchen to the main house. The house was one of the earliest structures built on Ridgewood, and for a long time it was considered the main foreman's house.

On the porch of the cookhouse, at the top of the stairs on the left side, was a wooden water well structure. The top lid was nailed down, but other than that, it looked ordinary enough. My Dad told me to never touch that well covering, or even go within two feet of it, ever. He said it could make people very sick, and many members of the Angle family that lived here had died from drinking the water in that well. We didn't know much more about the story until later, but my interest in that family started then. Long ago, as children living on Ridgewood, we would go to the little Angle Family cemetery on the ranch, walk through the gate bearing the little handmade sign that read:

"Welcome thou within my gate
Sit thee down and be at rest"

We would clean up the fallen branches and pull some weeds, and look at the dates on their granite headstones. I was intrigued by the Angle family who had once lived here, where I now lived. I had always wondered about the children who rested there, and why they all died so close together, and now I know; I have been in touch with direct descendants of that family.

About 1853 Rench Angle began acquiring ownership of the land where Ridgewood now stands. He acquired many pieces of adjoining property. He called the place "Ranch Angle". The Angle family became well known for their large land holdings and enjoyed the status of a well-to-do family.

In 1859, Rench Angle, age 31, took Mahulda Catherine Orender age 19, as his June bride, in Sonoma County, California. In 1860 they had their first child of the 15 children that they would eventually have over the next 23 years. They had nine boys and six girls. Nine of the children died young.

In 1878, Rench and Catherine lost six of their children who died within fifteen days of each other when they contracted diphtheria from their domestic water well that became contaminated. According to a Granddaughter of the first Angle child, that 18 year old daughter, Euphrasia Angle, helped her father bury all of her brothers and sisters lost in that tragedy. The small fenced and tree-shaded Angle Family cemetery is on a little rise in the middle of a field at Ridgewood, where it is tended to regularly.

In the following list of the Angle children, the dates are underlined of the ones who died of the diphtheria epidemic in 1878. At Mr. Angle's request, one little girl, an Indian child, who died in 1878 of diphtheria, is buried in the Angle cemetery, her grave unmarked. Many Angle family members rest in the Angle Family Cemetery on Ridgewood Ranch in the Walker Valley, most of them also being born in that same valley.

## The Angle Children

**1. Euphrasia Jane Angle** b. March 25, 1860 in the Walker Valley;
d. September 5, 1929 in Ukiah, California, at age 69.

**Married** E.L. Marrow, April 1880, in Mendocino Co. California

**Children of** Euphrasia and E. L. Morrow:

1. Eddie Morrow, b. in 1881; d. in 1890, in Mendocino County, California.

**Married** Charles Allen Aldrich, December 1886.

**Children of** Euphrasia and Charles Aldrich:

1. Alan Golden Aldrich b. February 1888 in Ukiah; d. 1942 in Napa County, California.
2. Winthrop B. Aldrich b. October 1899 in Ukiah; d. February 1957 in San Francisco County, California.
3. Helen A. Aldrich b. September 1891 in Ukiah; d. August 1966 in Sonoma County, California.
4. Sabin A. Aldrich b. May 1893 in Ukiah; d. May 1947 in Monterey County, California.
5. Marguerita B. Aldrich b. in March 1896 in Ukiah; d. May 1962 in Sonoma County, California.
6. James M. Aldrich b. January 1899 in Ukiah; d. April 1965.

**2. Anania (Annie) Angle** b. July 28, 1861 in Walker Valley; d. December 1919, at age 58.

**Married** Guy Hasket February 1885 in Mendocino County, California.

**Children of** Annie and Guy Hasket

1. Bertha Hasket b. February 1892 in Willits; d. March 1980 in Sonoma County.
2. Bessie Hasket b. January 1899 in Willits; d. November 1994 in Santa Rosa, California.

**3. David J.Angle** b.July 25, 1863 in Walker Valley, California; d.September 1, 1865 in Walker Valley at age 2 yrs, 1 mo.

**4. L.Ella Angle** b. March 9, 1865 in Walker Valley, California; d. **June 5, 1878**, at age 13, in Walker Valley, and is buried in the cemetery at Ridgewood Ranch.

**5. David F. Angle** b. November 26, 1866 in Walker Valley; d. January 9, 1867, at age 1 mo. 13 days, and is buried in the cemetery at Ridgewood Ranch.

**6. Franklin Angle** b. October 7, 1867 in Walker Valley; d. **June 12, 1878**, at age 11 yrs, 8 mos. in Walker Valley, and is buried in the cemetery at Ridgewood Ranch.

**7. Samuel H. Angle** b. September 12, 1868 in Walker Valley; d. **June 13, 1878** at age 9 years and 9 months, and is buried in the cemetery at Ridgewood Ranch.

**8. Ruben R. Angle** b. April 4, 1871 in Walker Valley; d. **May 30, 1878** d. May 30, 1878 at age 7 yrs, 1 mo. and is buried in the cemetery at Ridgewood Ranch.

**9. Ida M. Angle** b. February 1, 1873 in Walker Valley; d. August 1, 1875 at age 2 yrs, 6 mos. in Walker Valley, and is buried in the cemetery at Ridgewood Ranch.

**10.Rachael M. Angle** b. December 23, 1874 in Walker Valley; d. **June 6, 1878** at age3 yrs, 6 mos. in Walker Valley, and is buried in the cemetery at Ridgewood Ranch.

**11. M. Eva Angle** b. December 2, 1876 in Walker Valley; d. **June 7, 1878**, at age 1 yr, 6 mos. and is buried in the cemetery at Ridgewood Ranch.

**12. Carl Leon Angle** b. November 17, 1878 in Walker Valley; d. April 8, 1937 at age 58. Married Mabel Violet Benton on December 29, 1901, had one child.

**13.Joseph Victor Angle** b.April 27, 1880 in Walker Valley; d. August 1936 at age 56 and he is buried in Ukiah. Married Martha Belle Shore on June 29, 1911.

**14.Baslow Gustave Angle** b. April 15,1882 in Walker Valley; d. June 29, 1936 at age 54 and is buried in Ukiah, California.

**15.Richard Eugene Angle** b.September 25, 1883 in Walker Valley; d. July 23, 1950 at age 66 and is buried in Ukiah, California. He married Della Hammer on November 13, 1906.

<><><><><>

**Rench Angle died** on September 2, 1889 at the age of 61, in Walker Valley and is buried in the cemetery at Ridgewood Ranch.

**Catherine Orender (Angle) was married** to Sylvester Drew on July 1, 1891 in Mendocino County, California.

**Catherine Orender was married** to John Christy on June 18, 1907 in Mendocino County, California.

**Catherine Orender (Angle, Drew, Christy)** died on June 14, 1926, at age 86, in Ukiah, California.

**Family names** of descendants of the Angle family: Angle, Aldrich, Orender, Golden, Hasket.

## THE BUNK HOUSE AND THE RANCH HANDS.

Just across the road from the Lower Mare Barn was the bunkhouse. This was a place we girls were told to stay clear of. We might possibly overhear some loud foul language, or stories too colorful for the ears of young girls. Even from a proper distance, we did hear a loud cussword escape now and then. We just pretended we didn't hear it. One time, when the offending cowboy realized we girls were riding by within earshot of his salty remarks, he promptly came out of the bunkhouse toward us, and apologized profusely. We had not taken any particular offense or notice of his off-color words, but his apology made us feel like real ladies!

The other "no-no", according to our folks, was if we were lingering around the cookhouse porch when the ranch hands were there waiting for the cooks to ring the dinner bell that signaled a meal was on the table inside the dining hall. The hands in the summertime were mostly a hay crew of young college boys who seemed to be polite and friendly and harmless enough, but the very thought of them talking to us, in the form of socializing, seemed to make our Dads nervous. We didn't understand why then, because they brought their washed shirts to our house for us to iron them at 35 cents apiece, and that was acceptable. They were happy to have ironed shirts, and we were happy to have all the 35 cents spending money.

Once, to my dismay, when I was ironing a shirt for one of the summer haycrew fellows, I scorched it, leaving a brown iron print on the back of it. My Mom showed me how to remove some of the stain, but it didn't all come out. I felt so bad about ruining the shirt that I didn't want to accept any ironing money for it. The owner of the shirt, Ted, said it wasn't that bad, and would probably come out in the next wash, and he insisted on paying me for all the shirts anyway. An understanding fellow! That all came out fine, but my folks still said there was no hanging around talking with any of the boys in leisure time.

Two teenage girls came for a summer visit to stay with their relatives who lived on Ridgewood, and they got to know everyone. They weren't too interested in riding horses, but they liked the ranch. One of the girls was 16, and one day when we were riding around the ranch, double, on my horse, I asked her what it felt like to be all of 16. She looked at me, and said, "Not too much different from what it was like to be your age. It's just another year." I thought that one over for awhile, still not quite understanding what happens as you grow up another year. But later, I saw her "socializing" with one of the ranch hand guys, all by themselves, sitting in the tall grass out in the side yard of the main ranchhouse-cookhouse building! She told me, as I approached, that they were "just sitting in the grass talking". OK. But I couldn't see them at all when I first rode up. I guess what it means to be 16 is that you can socialize a little more like that.

## SHEEP

Just beyond the bunkhouse and across from the Lower Mare Barn was a sheep pasture. We found that the sheep were funny animals, behaving in strange ways and different from the horses and other animals. They seemed to have no personality; they were just sheep, wooly, short-legged sheep, who all ran in the same direction at the same time. They did everything as a group, one goes and they all go. It was a rare cattleman you would find that would eat mutton or lamb. But those sheep were there on the ranch, a part of it, making the livestock selection complete. And someone probably liked to eat lamb. Maybe the English Gardener did.

This flat sheep pasture had different kinds of trees and bushes in it unlike what grew on the rest of the ranch. This large bush, or short, no-trunk tree, whichever it was, had low spreading branches right on the ground like a jungle thicket. It was big around, and it offered a real choice place to build a new fort! A very shallow wide creek ran across the ground underneath these branches, making it even more interesting. We hollowed out little "rooms" in the thicket of those bushes, and in between chasing the curious sheep out of our fort again and again, we established quite a network of secret hiding places within it. The bush was so dense that we couldn't be seen by anyone passing by. It was a special place to us, someplace we didn't play often, but it was really nice when we went back there. When we did go back there to play, we found ourselves again reconstructing our rooms where the sheep had knocked the branches down. They liked it, too, and in our absence, they had obviously explored our fort, and it smelled like they had even slept there!

We did have fun raising the bummer lambs there on the ranch. The bummers were little newborn lambs that were maybe not getting enough milk from their moms, or maybe she had too many lambs to feed , or maybe she wouldn't take a particular lamb for some unknown reason. Sometimes a ewe died in giving birth, and then the baby lamb would go to another ewe and try to get milk. That usually didn't work. So this gave us kids the job of raising the bummers. We took the tiny baby lambs home and snuggled them in a blanket-lined laundry basket or box that was placed on the floor in back of the wood stove. If it was real cold, we put their bed on the open oven door. Sometimes we had two or three lambs at a time, and they helped to keep each other warm. They seemed comforted by each others company, too.

We fed them a bottle with a few ounces of warm milk often, even through the night, when they were so tiny. Soon they would let out a tiny little "baaaaaah" when they saw us coming with the bottle, and they became really enthusiastic about slurping up every last drop of milk. As they began to gain weight, we gave them fewer feedings with larger amounts of milk. When they began climbing out of their basket, and were standing up and walking good, we put them in a little pen outside. Mom said that having little lambs trotting around inside the house was not good! Being outdoors in the sunshine seemed to make them grow even faster. They were so cute to watch when they were running and playing. When they were old enough to eat hay and grain, we took them back to the other sheep pasture where they would grow up with the other lambs.

My brother became attached to one lamb that he named Danny. The lamb thought John was pretty special, too. We kept Danny around quite awhile, and he and John became great pals. John was preschool age at that time, and young animals and young children usually hit it off real well.

## SHEEP SHEARING TIME AT THE LOWER BARN

When it was time to shear the sheep as hot weather approached, it was done at the lower barn, The Sheep Barn, which was a tall old wooden structure that stood out in a field apart from the rest of the ranch. It was located south of the main headquarters across a large section of hayfields, up on a small rise. The creek ran nearby through the west side of the fields and on past to the Blue Clay Hills where it joined up with the creek that came out of The Wager Place.

The sheep shearers that came to do their job were a temperamental lot, and rather gruff. They preferred not to have an audience; they just wanted to get in there, get their shearing job done, get paid, and go on to the next job. They sheared each sheep fast, turning the animal this way and that as they held them up on their back legs, sometimes roughly, out of necessity to get the job done. We watched as each sheep's wooly coat was sheared off in huge clumps by the fast moving clippers. Their coats were sheared close to their skin, and were carefully guided by the experienced sheep-shearer's hands. The sheared wool was rolled up into bundles and tied, and then later transported to the wool buyer. The freshly shorn, naked looking sheep were turned out again, looking rather uncomfortable and lost for awhile with their lesser coat. But when the weather turned hot, they were glad to be free of their winter wooly coat!

## THE SWIMMING HOLE

The section of the creek that ran through the west side of the lower hayfields below The Sheep Barn was much deeper here than where it ran through the ranch headquarters. It had steeper banks here, and fewer accesses and crossings than where the same creek ran through the main part of the ranch. It was important to keep track of where the good creek crossings were, because you might find yourself on the other side of the creek with nowhere to cross when it was time to get home. It wasn't much fun to have to search for a place to cross, and you might look a long way to find one. That could make you late getting home, and then maybe subject to a scolding from Mom or Dad. The location of a good creek crossing often changed because of the winter storms.

There was a fine, quiet and secluded swimming hole in that part of the creek that stayed the same year after year. It had deep banks and a nice sandy bottom and was shaded by oak trees on both sides all day keeping it cool even on the hottest summer days. There was a good place to tie the horses up to the oak trees in the shade after we watered them in the creek. They were usually content to stand in the shade there while we swam and played in the creek for hours.

Sometimes we didn't have our swimsuits with us, if we hadn't planned to come by that way, but that didn't stop us. If it was a hot day, in we went, in the true skinny-dipper tradition. A couple of times, we heard noises in the bushes coming from the far side of the creek bank, and we wondered if someone was watching us swim. Just the cows, we thought, but we never knew for sure.

The worst thing that ever happened there was when I plunged into the creek with my new Mickey Mouse wristwatch on ... for the third time! I was so proud of that watch, I don't know how I could have forgotten to take it off. Mom had said that she wouldn't get it fixed if it ever happened again after the second time. She did get it fixed again, but didn't give it back to me until after swimming season passed, which was the whole summer.

## FRANKIE'S LOG CABIN

Upstream from the swimming hole, a log cabin was perched on the bank just above the creek on a bend where the water took a particularly treacherous turn. The rushing water went across some large logs and became what looked like a dark whirlpool. We never went swimming in this part of the creek.

The cabin was under oak trees, set squarely on the flat above the deep creek bank at the edge of the hayfields. High water had, at one time, eroded the bank away from under one corner of the cabin. This didn't seem to endanger the steadiness of the cabin, since it did not tip or lean in toward the creek. This cabin was supposed to be left alone, just as it was, nothing changed, forever. We were told that Mr. Howard's young son, Frankie, had built it with the help of his family. After Frankie's untimely death, Mr. Howard wanted the cabin left untouched. It had been one of Frankie's favorite places. In 1926, Frankie was killed in an accidental single-car roll-over on the ranch when he and two companions were coming back from a morning fishing trip up the creek. This, now, was about 1946. That tragic event twenty years or so earlier seemed like another world to us, but to the Howard family, it probably seemed like yesterday.

We just had to go in the cabin. Not wishing to harm anything, but so curious about Frankie's cabin, we finally found a way in, after several times of going there and just looking through the windows. We went down into the creek below the cabin first, to look up at the exposed under-flooring of the corner of the cabin that was hanging over the creek bank. We wanted to see if it looked like there was any danger of the cabin toppling into the creek. We decided, in our young judgement, that it looked safe enough. And of course, we couldn't ask anyone else's opinion.

We discovered that day that the cabin door on one side could be pressed to open. Laverne pressed her shoulder against the upper part of the wooden door gently, while turning the door knob, and the door gave way ever so slightly. Up to now, we thought that door had been locked. She continued to slowly push the door open into the shadowy interior of the cabin. We were holding our breath, and the only sounds we could hear above our heartbeat was the squeak of the rusty door hinges. In we went, one at a time, on tiptoe. Laverne, then Betty, then I. We were in this magical place called Frankie's Cabin!

It was darker inside than outside, even in the daytime, because of all the shady oak trees around it. The small cabin windows did not let much light in. We were very

# Frankie

Little soul, gone so long
Echoes of a lonesome song
Of long ago, of other years,
Childhood laughter; then parent's tears.
But is he gone? Does his soul still roam
Across this land he once called home ...
Has he come back ... somehow ...
From where he was ... into the now?
Hunting ... fishing in a mountain stream,
A playful lad full of adventure and dream,
He loved life itself; and had love for his brothers.
He had a special love for his Father and Mother.
Is it possible, in the way that things be,
He could return some way to his family
In the soul of a horse who was a winner
And had spirit to spare, even as a beginner.
Intelligence, endurance, a champion's heart,
Frankie and Seabiscuit, loved from the start.

*Jani Buron*

John Bosko Collection

Frank R. Howard at Ridgewood Ranch at age 14

careful not to walk over to the corner of the cabin suspended over the riverbed, scolding each other if one of us got too close to the "bad" side.

We looked around the room as our eyes got adjusted to the low light. There was a pretty, decorative dark wooden trestle table placed in the center of the room, along with a couple of chairs. A double bed of sorts, complete with bedding and a light yellow bedspread, was in one corner. Some bookshelves were under the window facing the hayfields, with sunlight streaming in on them. It did look as if someone had just been there. It was almost as if a warm spirit still lived there. It definitely wasn't a cold feeling. It just felt different inside that building than it did outside, like a world apart. We always felt bad that Mr. Howard lost his son on the same place where we had such fun. It didn't seem fair, somehow.

## THE JUNGLE

West of the swimming hole, a trail led on to what we called "The Jungle". The hayfield flats narrowed down west of the point where The Sheep Barn was on the knoll. The creek ran narrower, and the terrain became a flat bottom, narrow canyon. There was more greenery, more dense brush, and fewer oak trees. The trail was well defined, and it was the only trail in that part of the canyon. The further you rode, the narrower it got, and the denser the greenery got.

Soon you were surrounded by thick underbrush and swinging vines that looped from tree to tree. Some of the vines had leaves like grapevines, and even had small bunches of little green clusters that would become grapes. Guess they were wild grapes. The creek was under all that brush, somewhere, but you couldn't see it. We could swing from the vines, but not very far. We would get a good hold on a vine, then back up to get a good start, and swing out as far as we could. The small vines usually deposited us on the ground far short of our goal. We had visions of swinging through the jungle like Tarzan. Our patient horses looked on, thinking probably that these Tarzan games were all a lot of nonsense. When other kids came to the ranch to visit and we showed them The Jungle, they thought the place was quite unique. However, our friend Lee Persico was visiting the ranch one day and went with us three girls on horseback all the way out to The Jungle, and he was not impressed about playing Tarzan!

## THE BLUE CLAY HILLS

Beyond the jungle in a southerly direction were the "Blue Clay Hills." We were strictly forbidden to ride there, or even to go near it. The Jungle was as close as we went to those hills. The Blue Clay Hills lay between The Jungle and The Wager place to the south, and they were very visible from the 101 Highway. The Wager Place was where the Ridgewood roundups were held. But if you were in The Jungle, you couldn't ride there from here. If you rode to The Wager, it was on a different trail further West that took off from the ranch in a different direction and went around the back of the Blue Clay, completely avoiding that area. It was a good trail, and an old one. It had been established long ago when the people who lived at Leonard Lake would ride from their place to Ridgewood Ranch to pick up their mail.

We were restricted from riding into the Blue Clay because of the unsteady ground that was always moving, and the many caves and deep, hidden, bottomless holes in that territory. "Very dangerous," Dad said, "and a long way from help." It was at the edge of the Ranch property. One day as Dad was going by on the Highway, he saw me riding on a hill near there, in that area, but quite far from the Blue Clay, not even headed in that direction. But even that was too close, and was worthy of a good scolding when I got home.

## THE WAGER PLACE AND LEONARD LAKE

The Wager Place was located on the road now called Reeves Canyon that turns off Highway 101 a few miles south of the main Ridgewood entrance gate. It was a part of Ridgewood property. That road ends up at Leonard Lake, which was off Ridgewood property. That lake was very pretty, with trees along the shoreline. It was an all-day ride going across the hills from Ridgewood to that lake, and we girls did that sometimes. Other times we went there by car. Some of my distant relatives who were early settlers in Mendocino County had farmed property around the lake at one time. They moved on, and a little lady named Mrs. Nunes (or Noones, pronounced "Newness") lived there when we were at Ridgewood. She was a short lady, and had kind of reddish hair that framed her round smiling face. She was so cheerful and friendly, and seemed ageless, and was always so glad to see us come and visit. As far as we knew, she lived there at the lake year round. If the winter was wet or snowy enough to make the road out to the highway impassable by car, then she rode her horse and led a pack-horse out to get supplies.

On the road to Leonard Lake, still on The Wager, there was a little single-walled board cabin built many years ago, just uphill off the road. It was very weather-worn, and had been unused for a long time. Perhaps it belonged to one of the earliest settlers to arrive there, or maybe it was a line shack, or maybe remnants of a former hunting camp. It stood alone, with no other signs of corrals or barns near it. It was taller than it was wide, and had a slightly peaked roof.

Jani Buron Collection

Charles Howard's quarter circle H brand being used at a Ridgewood Ranch branding

Inside, it was very small, with just two little rooms with a door-sized opening in the wall between. In the far room an old rusted bedspring was on the floor in one corner. The walls were lined with many layers of newspapers that had been pasted on and used for insulation against the cold winters in that canyon. Some of the papers were still readable, in the old typeset of the day, and we found it interesting to look at some of the articles. We became interested in just how far the dates went back, and we carefully peeled back the top one to get to the next one, to see who could find the oldest date. Early 1900's is the oldest that we found. We had always hoped to find one dated from the 1800's.

One day when we rode up over the hill and started down to that cabin, we were stopped short by the sight of two horses tied up to the cabin that we thought no one ever went to. Upon a closer look, we recognized the two horses as belonging to two people from Ridgewood. No one was around anywhere outside the cabin. We rode on in another direction, and when we rode back, the horses were still tied up there. No going to the cabin that day. When we went back there later on, we saw no sign that anyone had been there, so those two riders did not leave any traces of their presence behind them.

The Wager Place was where the Ridgewood roundups were held when Ray Kane was the ranch foreman. The corrals were on a gently sloping hillside that went down to the banks of a creek. The younger kids spent most of the day playing down in the creek, wading and catching pollywogs. To cool off, we also drank the delicious, incredibly cold sodas kept on ice in the large galvanized washtubs that were partly submerged in the creek under overhanging shade trees.

The ranch hands and others who came to help, and the older kids who had horses, worked hard all day roping and branding and marking and doctoring the calves. It was fast, hard, dusty, hot, fun work. Lots of camaraderie, and the satisfaction of a necessary and important job well done at the end of the day. The women who weren't working in the corrals brought food out for everyone after the work was all done, and it was time to relax and cool off. As the sun was going down and marked the close of day, a campfire was started to barbecue a grill full of fine Ridgewood beef steaks. The wonderful aroma of campfire smoke and steaks cooking drifted across the small meadow, and all through the canyon, mingling with the sounds of laughter, happy voices, old and young, an occasional horse whinny, and cows mooing.

Roundups were and always have been an important social affair in the history of ranching. At each roundup, stories are told around a campfire, greatly embellished stories about previous roundups, and great rides, and wrecks, stories that grow. Then,

Lee Persico Collection

Ridgewood Roundup Dinner

The evening of the 1948 spring branding at a dinner a few of the folks invited are pictured here. Front row, left to right, are Mrs.J. W. Britton, Dr. J. W. Britton, Don Coleman, Lee Persico Jr., and young John Griffith. Back row, standing, Kenneth H. Colley Jr., Mrs. V. G. Smith, V. G. Smith, Mrs. Lee Persico, Mrs. Donald Coleman Mrs. Chet Griffith. Chet Griffith, Lee Persico. Seated are Miss Jani Griffith and Chuck Persico

always, a soft word or two is said in fond remembrance of those favorite people who are not here working the roundups with us anymore. It is a time for meeting, and greeting, and catching up on news of neighbors, and reminiscing, and bonding.

Later, when Ray Kane left as foreman and John Britton took over as the new foreman at Ridgewood, the roundups were moved from The Wager up to the corrals by The Upper Mare Barn at the north end of the ranch compound. There was no creek to play in there, but by that time I was old enough to go in the corrals and work the cattle, and I had my own horse, Billy the Kid, to ride, sometimes with a saddle, sometimes without. It was really a challenge to stay balanced on him bareback when he cut quickly for a stray cow on his own!

One year I caught the German measles from the Britton family's little boys, Johnny and Mike, that I baby-sat for there on the Ranch. The measles broke out on me just before branding day. My Mom said I had to stay home and indoors because of the danger of bright sunlight doing permanent damage to the eyes. Missing the branding day to me was like missing out on Christmas, Easter, and everything else fun. On the second day of the branding, I was allowed to go to the corrals with dark glasses and a hat on, and had to stay quietly in the shade. I couldn't ride and work cows, but at least I could watch. That alone made me better, just being there and watching the activities.

The women still brought lots of good food to this new location, and here we mostly tailgated it for the noonday meal; and we had no evening campfire barbecue. Sometimes we went to Doc and Pat Britton's house afterward for a social hour and story telling and more eating. There was usually a frying pan full of mountain oysters, or calf-fries, cooking on the kitchen stove. This made good material for quite a few jokes, especially if any city folk happened to be there. Someone usually remembered to take group photos at these gatherings, and they are a good documentation of who was there in what year, and of the Ridgewood gang and friends of long ago.

## GATHERING CATTLE OFF THE RANGE

Prior to the roundup, the gathering up of C. S. Howard's Hereford cattle that spread across the grazing land all over the ranch was a big, concerted effort, and was fun! We saddled up early, took a sack lunch, and headed out for the range at first light. Each group of riders took a different direction. The cows were brought in to a closer smaller pasture until it was time to take them to the actual corrals where they would get

Jani Buron Collection

Cattle drive on Ridgewood Ranch in the early spring. Jani is on the white horse

branded and inoculated for diseases. This process took a few days, and if we girls were lucky, we could get in on a couple of these roundup rides.

Riders spread out and went to the far reaches of the ranch, and started hunting for the white-faced red Hereford cows and their calves. Most of the cows would herd home real good, but there was an occasional pair determined not to go home that would dart out of the bunch and into a thicket of tall bushes so dense you couldn't even see which way they went. This kind was usually trouble all the way back to the corrals. There was some kind of rough brush to spur your horse through to get a runaway cow, most often not on flat ground, and of course, the rest of the herd kept moving on. Once you retrieved the renegade cows, you quickly pushed them up to join the rest of the herd, as fast as you could go and still keep them headed in the right direction. If a calf took off alone from the herd and you went after it, you had to watch where the mother cow was and be sure you didn't get between her and the calf, or you then became her prime focus, and her target. Mad Mama cows are nothing to be reckoned with.

One time when I went after a runaway cow and calf that sped away from the herd past me, and into the brush on a sidehill, my Dad, concerned for my safety, shouted at me, "Let 'er her go!". However, my horse and I were already committed in a downhill run in that direction, and we had to keep going. Dad directed the closest rider to go over to help me, but I was able to get that pair out and headed back to the herd all on my own. Billy the Kid worked so good, and was I proud! So was Dad, in his own quiet way.

At the end of the day, by the time the cowboys gathered all the cows together and we headed for home, everyone was tired, hungry, and thirsty; the cows, the people, the horses, and the cow dogs. It was a quiet, low-key trip back to the ranch headquarters. We rode along the dusty road back to the ranch in the end-of-the day setting sunlight, just keeping the herd together and moving them slowly toward the ranch headquarters. Some riders would have to go back for the stray cows still out there, but not today.

## "THE LAKE"

One section where we went to gather up the cows was beyond the ranch lake, I suppose called Walker Lake, but we always just called it "The Lake". It was a large, long lake, about a half mile wide and three-quarters of a mile long, formed by a large cement dam going across a deep canyon. It was spring fed, and the water was always cool and clean. The dam had a deep spillway that emptied into the creek below Walker Lake that went through Ridgewood.

Fred Finke photos

Walker Lake on Ridgewood Ranch in the 1930's showing the boat house

Mr. Howard had built a nice boathouse where the boats were always kept inside out of the weather. Inside the boathouse, the boats were put on a boat-carrier frame by a large sling. Then they were launched into the lake by a kind of a mechanically operated hand winch system that operated a little trolley, and let the boats down a long sloped ramp directly into the lake beside the covered "U"-shaped dock. The boats were pulled back up again by using the same method in reverse. Mr. Howard had quite an assortment of boats; speedboats, rowboats, canoes, kayaks, and even a bicycle-pedal-pontoon boat. The "bicycle boat", as we called it, was a custom built water going vessel. It was an actual bicycle mounted on two pontoons, with a paddle somewhere in between underwater. Once launched, the "pilot" would then pedal the bike in a normal fashion, and this made the bicycle-pontoon boat glide across the water at whatever speed the pilot could make it go.

The area next to the docks of the boathouse was considered a nice place to swim. Out farther, the lake was deep and dark, and I felt safer staying close to shore so I knew where the bottom was while in the water. When I swam in The Lake as a child, I never felt comfortable in that cold dark water. I stayed near the edge at all times. I knew that all the creek and river swimming holes I swam in always felt better, no matter how cold and dark the water was in them.

I thought back to the time a few years earlier when we were living in Laytonville, a little town north of Willits. A playmate friend of mine, from the Harwood Family, about six years old, had drowned in one of our favorite swimming holes at his place. There was a narrow footbridge over that hole, and we walked across it to get to the shallower place to swim. We always went across the bridge with an adult holding our hand, and when I looked down into the water from that bridge, it looked deep and dark. We had been swimming there a couple of days before, and I wasn't there the day he drowned, but it sure left an impression on me about how sad everyone was. I missed him, too, and I didn't quite understand it all. But I knew to be careful about this swimming thing! His Mom was so sad whenever she saw me. She liked to see me, but I did remind her of their lost son. She was in the hospital giving birth to a new little daughter when they lost him. But here at The Lake, there was something more than that, something very mysterious about what I felt in that water. Laverne and Betty felt the same way, too.

Many years later, I learned that Mr. Howard had directed that dam to be built in order to form a lake to cover up the spot on the road where his young son Frankie had been fatally injured in a car accident. We girls knew that Frankie had his wreck on the road near The Lake, but never knew exactly where. We had imagined several locations where his car could have rolled over, but they were all wrong. The exact spot was actually under The Lake. Mr. Howard liked to fix things, to make them well, to heal up wounds, and so he had created The Lake, a happy place. The spot where the accident occurred would be out of sight forever, and would not serve as a constant reminder of the tragedy. It was a lovely spot on the Ranch, nice to fish in, pretty to ride around it, and attracted lots of wildlife to its shores.

## THE BICYCLE BOAT

One day when a group of us from the Ranch went up to The Lake, we were checking out the boathouse, and my Dad became intrigued by the bicycle pontoon pedal boat, and he wanted to try it out on The Lake. There was some discussion about if it worked, and if they should use it, and if so, how to get it onto the launching ramp. After all the decision making, there was much tugging and pulling and sweating and laughing, and the grown-ups finally got the pedal boat to the launching ramp and then into the water. A couple of men held onto the handlebars from the dock, and Dad jumped on the thing.

The first thing Dad learned as he jumped on was that you had to stay in the middle of the bicycle to stay balanced and upright. Then he began pedaling, and making forward motion on the water out onto The Lake, as the rest of the party looked on from the dock. It worked real well for awhile.

As we watched from the dock, we noticed that Dad and the bicycle boat began to have a lower profile in the water. When Dad's feet began to splash the water as he was pedaling, he looked down and discovered that the pontoons were slowly taking on water. He was sinking! His friends on shore were shouting to him that he was sinking, and to turn around and come back, quick. The added weight of the lake water leaking into the pontoons was making it harder and harder to pedal. He did manage to get the pedal boat turned around and then pedaled as hard as he could to get back to shore. People were reaching out from the dock to help Dad when he got close enough; that is, those who were not overcome with laughter at the strange sight of the sinking pedal boat and the frantic rider. They were cheering him in, with hands outstretched to help him when he got back to the dock. "Only a little ways to go, Chet, keep pedaling!" "We're here for you!" More peels of laughter.

He was laughing, too, at himself and the whole situation, all the while pedaling as fast as he could, while sinking! He did make it back to the docks without totally sinking. Several of the menfolk grabbed the handlebars to keep the heavy waterlogged bicycle pontoon-boat afloat while Dad jumped off and back onto the dock. He was relieved to be safely onshore again, and nothing worse had happened than Dad's boots getting waterlogged and his jeans getting soaked.

The men managed to keep the nose of the bicycle boat above water and afloat, even though it kept wanting to sink. They wrestled it through the water and around the end of the dock and got it to rest safely on the foot of the launching ramp. The men let out a collective sigh of relief when they got it that far, and then took a break before going any farther. It wouldn't do to have that bicycle boat go to the bottom of The Lake. It might be one of Mr. Howard's favorite things , since he had been a bicycle repairman in his early years. He may even have designed it. Now the only problem was getting the pedal boat up higher on the launching ramp so the pontoons could drain. With that done, it then needed to get back up into the boathouse where it could continue drying out. What a story this made! It was retold over and over, bringing laughter each time, especially from my Dad!

## THE LAKE SPILLWAY

While at The Lake, we girls used to walk out on the dam to the flood gate controls where we pretended like we were the "watergate-master". We put our hands on the gate wheels and made them move just a little bit, one way and the other. We could look down into the big spillway from there. It was usually dry in the center, and had a wet mossy covering down each side from the tiny water leaks in the dam watergates. We were never supposed to go down in the spillway in case someone might let the water come rushing out, not knowing we were in there. Since we knew that we were the only ones there at The Lake that day, and we were feeling adventurous, we thought it would be safe to go down in the spillway, just to walk down it and come out on the creek at the bottom.

Laverne agreed to hold our horses while Betty and I scrambled down over the slanted outer walls to the floor of the spillway. We immediately encountered the slippery moss at the sides of the spillway on the downhill slope, and had trouble keeping our footing on the slanted cement in our slick leather-soled western boots. Suddenly we realized that we couldn't hang on to the sides to keep ourselves up, and we couldn't climb out of the thing, either. It was a long way to the bottom, longer than it had looked from the top, and we began to get scared. As we slipped and slid around on the watery moss, we realized that this was why we weren't supposed to go down into the spillway!

Laverne, being the older sister and more sensible, called to us from the banks of the spillway to get out quick, and what a foolish thing it was to do, going down there. We knew that already. Panic began to set in. Maybe when we pretended to turn the watergate wheels, and they had actually moved ever so slightly, we really did make it work, and water might come cascading down on us at any minute and wash us down the creek! At that thought, we tried scrambling up the sides again, and that didn't work. We then went as quickly as we could, balancing carefully, down the dry center of the steep spillway slope to the bottom, inching our way along so as not to fall. We found that the slippery moss was at the bottom, too, and the drop to the creek was a long one, right onto the big rocks below. What a fix we were in!

Finally we decided to take one more try at the spillway walls. We backed up across that wide spillway and took a good run at the walls, somehow scrambling over the slick wet moss and up the rough cement walls. We were so glad to get out of there and to be safe on the topside once again! We vowed to never to go down there again. I don't recall telling anyone else about it right away, either!

## WINDY GAP

Beyond The Lake, the hills went up steeply and became quite rugged, and the trail became narrower. If you knew where to go, and which forks to take, you would end up at this unusual place due West of The Lake called Windy Gap. The hills were round and tall, and not too heavily wooded. As you approached the Gap, it was quiet, because the prevailing wind came from the other side of the hill, from the direction of the Pacific Ocean, miles away. The Gap was a narrow, worn, "U" shaped cutout in between two of the highest hills in that ridge. When you stepped into the Gap, the wind speed was incredible. It hit you and your horse with top speed, and you both had to brace yourself to stay upright. It blew the hearing out of your ears, tore at your jacket and pants, and if you forgot to tie your hat on, it instantly sailed off into the distance over the canyon below. We usually remembered to hand our hat to someone else to hold for safekeeping before we rode into The Gap. It blew your breath back into your throat, along with any words you might try to spit out! It blew your eyes shut. The constant wind blew and whistled in your ears until you couldn't stand it anymore, at which point you retreated back to the safety of the off-wind hillside, where your senses worked again. The horses were always glad to get out of it, too. It blew like this constantly, day and night.

The wonder of it all, and the reason for riding up here, is that you could see the Pacific Ocean from here! If you could step out into the Gap, stand the wind, and open your eyes a little crack, and look West on a clear day, there off in the distance was the ocean! The howling wind came off that ocean and funneled through The Gap at tremendous speeds. It is said that this is what gave the Walker Valley its special climate, warmer in the Wintertime, and cooler in the Summertime. The distant ocean was an awesome sight to see at the end of a challenging ride, well worth the trip up there.

## STRANGE NOISES IN THE WOODS

The road to The Lake was a good road, in most places nice and flat and smooth. It was a nice two-mile walk from our house, which in turn was about one half-mile from the ranch headquarters. The road wound around through some pretty countryside, and gently climbed upward to The Lake.

On that road to The Lake, when I was riding alone one time and was just approaching the dam, my horse Billy the Kid suddenly stopped in the middle of the road and took notice of something ahead of us. I didn't see anything on the road ahead. He seemed to be concerned about something on the wooded hillside to the left, just across the road from the grassy flats above the banks of the creekbed. I looked around everywhere, seeing nothing out of the ordinary. He still insisted there was something moving in the woods. Then I heard a rustling noise in the dry leaves of the hillside. Billy didn't want to go any further, but I urged him on for a few steps. He danced sideways down the road, staying as far away as possible from the shadowy woods, turning his neck way around looking in back of us, and keeping his eyes wide open on whatever was making the noise. Silly little bug-eyed horse, I thought to myself. Probably just a little bird or a squirrel, or maybe even a rabbit.

Then I saw it! A mountain lion! And he saw us! He was eating on a deer carcass under the trees right near the road and when he heard us coming, he had begun covering the carcass up with dry leaves to hide it from other predators and from us. This also keeps it cool from the hot summer days. I was stunned and fascinated at the sight, and wanted to stay and watch more of the lion's activities, but Billy was really anxious to get out of there. The lion bounded away quickly and disappeared into the shadows of the woods, but Billy only partly relaxed. No doubt he sensed we were in the lion's territory, and the lion may still be here, and he didn't want to challenge him. We rode on to The Lake without further incident, but on our return trip, Billy was very jumpy and bug-eyed as we rode past that same spot. He insisted on going in a wide circle off the far side of the road from where the lion had been visible earlier. He knew more about the danger than I did.

One time earlier when we had been out riding up the steep slopes of Lion Mountain, I was trying to get Billy to go up, over and around a big log that was across the trail. He kept refusing to go any further. I was riding bareback, so I slid off to walk and lead him on up the trail. As my feet touched the ground I looked down and saw a large fat rattlesnake coiled up under the log in a place where I couldn't see him from horseback. But Billy knew he was there, and he was trying to warn me of the danger. He was so glad when I scrambled back on him and we headed down the hill fast!

## THE REDWOOD TREE GOOSEPEN

On that same road to The Lake, out in a flat field across the fence from the pear orchard, stood a goosepen of Redwood trees. They were old trees and young trees, together, growing in a tight circle. Inside the circle it was like a little room with a green roof cathedral of Redwood branches. The floor was a soft cushion of fallen Redwood needles and small soft branches. This made a perfect, prefabricated fort! While we played there, the horses were content to be tied up in the shade, or better yet, to be let loose to graze on the tender green grasses that grew near the trees. That Redwood stand was ageless, and so quiet and cool in the summer. It stood serene and silent through the ages, like an everlasting landmark of time. It has seen all that ever went on in the Walker Valley, long before we were there, and will witness whatever happens long after we are gone. If only the trees could talk.

## THE RESERVOIR AND THE TRAIN TRACKS

The trail to the reservoir headed east out of Ridgewood proper, and went under Highway 101 through a little tunnel, which we always found to be fun to pass through on horseback. Then on up to the reservoir, and if you were going that far, you might as well go all the way up to the train tracks at Howard Station and see what was going on with the train. In order to get over Ridgewood Grade, these trains often had two or three locomotives in the front end, and maybe three pushing on the back end.

At the roundhouse, we could watch the locomotives get on the round turntable, and be turned around and put back on the track to be used in the other direction. Laverne, Betty and I would sit on our horses near the train tracks and watch the train coming slowly up the grade. It went slower and slower, sometimes looking as if it would stop, heaving and puffing, just barely crawling. Then when it got to more level ground near the summit, it took a deep chugging breath, and the engine inhaled new life, and the train began moving a little faster. The chain reaction of the train boxcar hitches each re-adjusting to a different speed on down the line made an interesting evenly spaced heavy clicking sound, all the way to the last car, like a standing row of dominoes each knocking the next one down. Now the train once again had command of its own speed, having struggled up to reach the top of the mountain and traveled over this fearsome grade.

In the wintertime, it was an inspiring sight to see the great clouds of steam rising from the locomotives in front of the snowy mountains against a great blue sky. The powerful earthshaking sound of the train engine working to get up the grade, and then the clear glorious sound of the whistle, telling the world, "We made it!" The horses were interested, too, looking, watching, and moving their ears forward and back to take it all in. Sometimes a loud unexpected train whistle caught them by surprise and would make them jump a little. Now in 2004 the train tracks are still there but the trains are no longer running. Many things from the past that were so awesome have been replaced in the name of progress.

Whenever we girls rode up to the Howard train station, we sometimes took in the whole mountain if it was a nice sunny day. We checked out the trails and the special places. On one of those days when noontime came around, we were looking for some shade to tie up the horses and have our lunch. As we were riding along, we came upon an old wooden picnic table. Then we noticed a little wooden cupboard nailed up on a nearby tree, and a shelf built between two trees that probably served as the camp kitchen counter. We also noticed a ring of rocks where a campfire had been.

This was someone's Fall hunting camp! What an ideal place to do lunch! We got off our horses and tied them up to one of the little oak trees. Then we spread our treats out on the table and ate, and looked in the cupboard that had a few supplies in it, and generally enjoyed the hospitality of the little camp. We left a dated note in the cupboard thanking whoever's camp it was for the use of the table, and said we lived at Ridgewood, and signed our names. When we were back that way later, we checked out the place again. Upon opening the cupboard to see if our note was still there, we found an answer to our note saying we were welcome to use the place anytime and thanks for leaving the note!

From the top of this mountain, you could look back down and see the whole Walker Valley that lay below. The Ridgewood Ranch headquarters was placed in the center like a large shining jewel. Further up the hill to the North, Highway 101, the Redwood Highway, emerged at the top of the grade on the East side of the canyon across from Big Rock Candy Mountain, and then it dropped on down the steep and twisty route, carrying travelers past the distinctive Ridgewood Ranch entrance gate at the bottom of the grade, and on down to Ukiah. To the West, the heavily timbered distant coast range lay beyond the Ranch, and past that, the Pacific Ocean. This mountain is where Windy Gap is

Jani Buron Collection

Ridgewood snow, with Redwood Grove and Lion Mountain in the background

located, a narrow pass through the mountain where the fresh breezes from the ocean continually blow through. What a paradise of varied landscape, vast spaces, open skies, and greenery! What a feast for the eyes! Even our horses looked at the view with interest, and drew deep breaths and snorted, nodding their heads, as if in approval of all they saw.

## SNOW

The snow came to Ridgewood in many different ways, and it didn't happen every winter. If it snowed enough to make traveling on the Ridgewood Grade hazardous, then, of course, we didn't have to go to school. If that part of the highway was even the slightest bit slick, it greatly increased the chances of crashing into the guardrail and skidding over the precipitous outside edge of the road and go tumbling down into the canyon.

On those snow days, it was a joy to play in the fluffy white stuff. Sometimes it required several changes of clothes to stay reasonably warm and dry. If there was enough snow accumulation to make a snowman, that was really cause for celebration. If the snowline was up higher on the hills above Ridgewood, we could ride up there and check out the fresh layer of whiteness. It usually snowed heavier up by the train tracks. It snowed lots more in Willits, to the north of Ridgewood, at a higher elevation, than it did in Ukiah, to the south of it, and in a lower valley. Ridgewood, being right in between, got a pleasant mixture of the two climates. We knew that if we had snow at Ridgewood, then Willits had a lot more snow, and the roads were slick, and sometimes the schools there were even closed.

## WILLITS VS. UKIAH

The fact that the entrance to Ridgewood Ranch was located on the 101 Highway, almost equidistant between Willits and Ukiah, was of constant concern to each town's Chamber of Commerce. Each community wanted to have the claim to fame of being the home of Charles S. Howard's Ridgewood Ranch, and the world famous Seabiscuit. At some point, Mr. Howard made it clear that Willits was the community that Ridgewood belonged to. Depending on what town a journalist was associated with, Ridgewood was referred to as being "North of the town of Ukiah", or as being "South of the town of Willits".

We went to Willits for all of our general supplies and for social activities. The rare trip to Ukiah, a much larger city, might be for the initial purchase of fall school clothes, or some items that might be found only in the larger Ukiah stores. Once there,

Jani Buron Collection

Mr. Howard placed this billboard on Hwy 101, note "Horses for Sale"

it was an all day trip, and we made all the stops in many stores. Ukiah had warmer summer days than Willits did, and it didn't always cool off in the evening, so our September shopping trips were usually very hot.

## RIDGEWOOD HIGHWAY BILLBOARDS

### Grandpa and Grandma

The other event that took us to Ukiah was when my Grandpa occasionally invited all the family down for a grand Holiday dinner at the Palace Hotel. We all sat at a big long table covered with fancy white tablecloths, and ate from the hotel's finest china plates with real silver place settings. Grandpa would order up an impressive spread, and always fussed to make sure everyone had enough to eat, and just exactly what they wanted. We young cousins sat up to the table properly, displaying the manners befitting our "dress-up" clothes, and enjoyed the feast Grandpa ordered up for us. We did miss having someone's back yard to run and play hide-and-seek in before and after dinner, but at the same time we felt so special as we enjoyed Grandpa's fine treat in the Hotel's elegant dining room.

When we were at Ridgewood, my Grandma lived in Hopland, a very small town south of Ukiah. She taught grade school there. They had hired her on a full time contract when she was almost 60, much to her astonishment. World War II had made it necessary for the younger women of the nation, some of who were teachers, to go to work in the defense plants, so the schools turned to the older teachers to return to their teaching positions.

Grandma was so happy to be needed again, and so loved teaching all the little children about nature and music and wonders of the world, beyond what was in the text books. And the town of Hopland loved her. The townspeople embraced her and watched over her, coming to her aid whenever she was in need. After her little house burned to the ground, and after her school burned, too, the townfolk provided her with the replacement of all household goods, tenfold, and saw to her other daily needs, as well. Grandma was always used to doing for others, and she was quite touched with this loving response from her community, never realizing just how deserving she was of all this attention.

One of Grandma's greatest joys was coming to Ridgewood for visits with us for Holiday dinners, or a weekend, or during the summer vacation time. She caught the Greyhound bus in Hopland, and notified us ahead about what time the bus would be dropping her off at the Ridgewood Ranch gate on Highway 101. She got off the bus and waited there for us, sitting on her up-ended suitcase. We would drive out and pick her up and take her back to our house, about two miles into the ranch. She made quite a sight, a little elderly lady happily sitting on her suitcase at the edge of the dirt ranch-road waiting for us, under that grand entrance gate to Ridgewood. The Ridgewood gate was made of two vertical Redwood logs on each side of the entrance road, with a single log connecting across the top to make an archway. Across the top of the horizontal overhead log was the sign announcing "Ridgewood Ranch, Home of Seabiscuit". A split rail fence along the highway leading up to the gate on either side made it stand out and look even larger. A small "Visitors Welcome" sign stood in the ground to the left of the gate.

Grandma told us that as she traveled up the 101 Highway on the way to Ridgewood, she watched for the large billboard sign that Mr. Howard had put up by the road announcing to all passersby that this was Ridgewood Ranch, Home of Seabiscuit. He was so proud of his horse and his ranch. This was a large wooden sign painted white, with red lettering, facing the highway, and it was planted firmly in Ridgewood soil near the southern property line. Another one just like it was at the northern border of the ranch facing Highway 101. She said it always gave her heart a start, because she knew the bus would soon be at the Ridgewood gate, and she would be seeing us.

Grandma loved being on a ranch again with the hayfields and horses and cows and hills and trees. She and Grandpa had owned a large ranch for many years, located halfway between Ridgewood and the Pacific coast. Grandpa was born there, as were all of his children. We grandchildren spent lots of time there, too. The whole family enjoyed many happy years on that place. That Philbrick Ranch in Comptche was gone now, but Grandma still needed her connection with country to feel whole again. Ridgewood provided that satisfying, comforting connection. In the 1800's my Grandpa's father had ridden from Comptche across the Ridgewood hills to the North Hunting Ground Ranch in search of good beef cattle for his butcher shop. He met my future Great-Grandmother there, on that ranch next to Ridgewood, that was then called "Ranch Angle". Rench and Catherine Angle and their large family lived there at that time.

The big sign at the south end of the ranch that Grandma used to wait to see still stands, with paint peeling and rather neglected, beside an old abandoned portion of Highway 101, The Redwood Highway. It is a reminder of another day, when things were newer and fresher. It was a significant beginning of life's journey for so many of us, in a gentler time. It still looks proud in a weather-beaten sort of way, and is a remnant of glorious days gone past. It is not seen by the highway travelers of today, and so few of us know just where to look for it.

## EAGLE PEAK

Eagle Peak stands tall and proud and is the highest part of a mountain ridge west of Ridgewood. It always beckoned, looked intriguing and promised of great adventure. As children, we made plans to climb it. I talked about climbing it and said one day we would climb it. Well, one day that opportunity came about, and quite suddenly. Hubert, Laverne and Betty's older brother, said he would take us up there, right now, today, while he was home. Wow! We hurriedly got together a lunch with their Mom's help, then we dressed in our warm clothing, good rubber boots and took warm jackets. The plan was to get as close as we could by car, then hike up to the top and eat our lunch. The weather was fall-like and cloudy, so getting too hot wouldn't be a factor. The folks gave us instructions on safety procedures and directions. They said, "Be home before dark", and we were off. How exciting!

Hubert drove the car around to the roads he knew that led to the base of Eagle Peak. It was all new country to us girls. The country looked quite different as we neared the mountain, and the landmarks changed in appearance. We kept looking out the car windows at landmarks along the way to keep our bearings straight. Hubert, being an older brother, knew a lot about this kind of stuff, so we relied on his planning.

We went as far as Hubert could drive the car, then he parked it and we got out, taking our supplies with us. We started up the nearest hill on foot, and since there were not many trails made on this mountain, we made our own trail as we went, with Hubert in the lead. We hiked up and up. A misty cloud began settling over us at the top of the first ridge. We figured that we had one more ridge to climb, then down into a draw, then up the next ridge to be on the same ridge as Eagle Peak. We went on up into the mist, and got to the top where we could see over it. It was then that we discovered that we had just spent a lot of time climbing the wrong ridge! Eagle Peak was way over there in a different direction. Hubert said we would barely have time now to make it back to the right ridge, get to the Peak, then back down in time, so lunch would have to wait. We girls were hoping to eat soon, but we did want to get to Eagle Peak like we had planned.

On we went, back down the wrong ridge that we were on, then up again, this time on the right ridge. The climb got steeper and steeper, and rockier, and Hubert kept encouraging us to keep going. He promised us a fine lunch on Eagle Peak. It got colder, and drizzly, but the hiking kept us warm, all except for our hands! Finally we arrived at the summit, and it looked so different in shape and size from the distant silhouette we had always seen from the Ranch. And we found caves in it! One cave was big enough for all of us to get in, which we did. Hubert built a small campfire inside the cave so we could

Jani Buron Collection

Eagle Peak on the center horizon, a landmark for miles in any direction

get our hands warm. Verna, their Mom, had sent cookies, and delicious little Vienna sausages in a can that we cooked on that campfire. Lunch tasted very special, and we got warm, and we had reached the top of Eagle Peak! We enjoyed our vista of Ridgewood, that lay below, and the other surrounding deep wooded canyons and steep peaks. We were all happy!

The trip back down to the car went very fast, mostly downhill, and just like barn-soured horses, we traveled faster going home! We had proud stories to tell the folks. We had made it to the top of Eagle Peak! We even had lunch over a campfire in a cave up there! Now we could look up at the Peak from the Ranch, and know what it looked like up close, and what the Ranch had looked like from there.

## BIG ROCK CANDY MOUNTAIN

The big rock at the north end of the ranch that is very visible from Highway 101 at the top of the Grade, is what we called Big Rock Candy Mountain. The old Ridgewood Grade looked up to it as the highway wound around the opposite side of the canyon between the two high points of the Rock and the Grade. The new section of the freeway that is travelled on today is higher, and almost looks straight across level at the top of the Rock.

This rock is straight up and straight down on three sides, with a rocky dome shaped top. From the west on the backside, there was a good horse trail that went further up toward the ridge where the rock jutted out. At the end of the trail, there was a good place to tie the horses up while we climbed on up to the top. This route left a steep but fairly short and easy climb to the top. We could make it up there in no time!

The fun was in standing on the top of Big Rock Candy Mountain and waving at the people in the cars across the canyon coming up the Ridgewood Grade. We would watch for someone to see us and wave back. Most people were concentrating on their driving and staying on the narrow road ahead, and making the sharp turns. Some did look around. When they saw us, they were so startled to see three little girls on top of that rocky peak waving at them! Some returned a big wave back to us out their car window.

We took numerous flags up there and erected them, securing the base with lots of rocks, but the flags always seemed to get knocked down eventually by the mountain goats or the winter winds. Hubert went up with us one time, armed with wire and tools, and he put up a flagpole that lasted for years. This sturdy pole far outlasted the next flags we put on it.

Jani Buron Collection

Big Rock Candy Mountain is what we called this peak where we raised our flags.

Going back down the mountain was always fun, if you remembered to take a cardboard up with you. There was a loose shale rock slide coming down off the west side of the mountain that we slid down on the cardboard. Staying on your cardboard was a trick, but it was sure a neat ride down if you could manage it! We stashed the cardboards at the bottom for future use, if they survived the ride down. The horses would hear us coming down the rock slide squealing and shouting back and forth, and they would be looking in our direction and watching for us when we came down the trail toward them. They were glad to see us, but can you imagine their conversation about "those silly girls!" while they were waiting for us!

Ridgewood Ranch parade group with Jani, Betty and Laverne on the 4th of July 1948

# Chapter 7

## WILLITS FRONTIER DAYS AND RIDING IN THE PARADE

The Willits Frontier Days Rodeo and parade was a big hometown July 4th celebration, and it was always fun. We made plans and looked forward to it all year. My Dad helped put on the rodeo, like everyone else, and took his turn as rodeo committee chairman. My Mom helped with the entries and rodeo secretary duties. In the beginning, the money made on Frontier Days went to the Howard Hospital fund, and so Doc Babcock was a big supporter, too. Started in 1926, it was, and still is, a big event in Willits and all of Mendocino County. It is billed as the oldest continuous Rodeo in California.

Charles S. Howard was the very first Grand Marshal for the first Frontier Days Parade. It is traditionally a two-day rodeo, but it has occasionally been a three day event, years ago! The related activities of the Jr. Rodeo, the Rodeo Sweetheart contest, the horse show, and the carnival take place all week. But the BIG day was the Fourth of July, with the parade, the barbecue feed, and the rodeo.

It seems that everyone came to town for the rodeo, even a man known as The Hermit. We saw him for years and never knew him by any other name. As far as we knew, he lived in the mountains somewhere, and would come out of the mountains into town for the Fourth of July Celebration. He would slowly ride his bicycle down Main Street in the parade, his long white beard flowing. He wore a kind of a buckskin robe outfit, and it always looked cleaned up some for the occasion. He smiled slightly, but I never heard him talk. After the 4th of July, he disappeared, but we could count on seeing him again next year if he survived the winter. We never knew just where he lived in the hills, although we might hear someone talking of him from time to time. He was a memorable sight, looking as though this was the highlight of his whole year!

Logging trucks were a part of the parade, each with their biggest and best Redwood log to show off. These huge logs were so big around that they made the big log trucks hauling them look like toy trucks as the log was carried down Main Street. Sometimes it took three trucks just to haul one tree. The tall tree was cut up into thirds, and each log section was placed on a truck.

David Bacci Collection.

"The Hermit" Henry Shaw was a colorful character around the coast

Beautifully decorated floats, horse drawn and motor driven, were in the parade, and lively marching bands and various marching groups, including military drill teams, family riding groups, and single entries of horse and rider. The city fire engines and Forestry fire trucks led the parade, followed by the Grand Marshal and various dignitaries.

Most ranches rode as groups in the parade, and Ridgewood Ranch was one of the biggest parade groups. We had lots of riders, and the stagecoach drawn by a fine team of horses, with Howard family members and friends riding inside. We wore our best jeans, white long-sleeved shirts, Western straw hats, and red satin ties, thus representing the Howard colors of red and white. The horses were bathed and their coats were oiled and their hooves were polished. The saddles and bridles were soaped and shiny. We were a proud and fine looking group!

The parade went south down Main Street witnessed by large and enthusiastic crowds standing on the sidewalks along the way. Then we turned down a small dirt street that came into the side of the rodeo grounds. We stayed in formation, and once on the racetrack we rode past the grandstand for those who preferred to sit in one place to view both the parade and the rodeo! They were always very appreciative, and clapped and cheered for us as we rode by.

Then it was rodeo time! We watered our horses, loosened up the saddle cinches, and then tied them up in the shade of the cool oak trees. That done, we went for a hamburger and a soda pop, at one of the booths under the backside of the grandstand. Then we were ready for the show to begin!

There was a racetrack all around the rodeo arena and stock pens in those years, and there was activity going on somewhere all the time, in any direction you looked. Some of the events taking place on the track directly in front of the grandstand were trail horse competition, color horse classes, stake races, and at some point during the rodeo, trick and fancy riding. At the same time, in the arena, cowboys and cowgirls competed in bareback riding, saddle bronc riding, calf roping, team roping, barrel racing, bull riding, and bulldogging, now called steer wrestling.

Three times a day they held "open" horse races around that racetrack, with a lap'n tap start. Lap'n tap start means that they line up to start the race without benefit of a starting gate; this is similar to the start that was used in the historical Seabiscuit-War Admiral match race in 1938. Now that was exciting, just getting a half-dozen horses all facing the right direction, side by side, on the track at the same time, and having both horse and jockey ready for the start altogether. A lot of scrambling and hollering went on

1930's racing at Willits, California with Dink Persico 1st. Jim Millerick 2nd

as the horses were jumping around, turning, prancing up and down, while chomping at the bit to run. The riders were trying to hold them fairly still in a forward position so they can get off to a good start. "Wait ... wait ... wait ..." ... "Whoa!" .... "Turn around!" ... "I'm not ready yet!" "OK! OK! Let's go!" When they are as ready as they are going to get, the gun shot quickly sounds and the rodeo announcer officially says, "They're off!". Sometimes in a cloud of dust, I might add! The horses jump forward and scramble for position as the announcer calls the race, if he can see it through the dust! The horses quickly go around the backside, and sometimes twice around. As they come around to the homestretch and down to the finish line, the crowd goes wild, so you can't hear the announcer anyway! After they cross the finish line in whatever order, the announcer tells the crowd who was first, second, and third. There are some smiles and some frowns, some money changes hands, and everyone has a good time. People start planning what to bet on in the next race.

Three races per day was the usual card, and the same horses could compete in any or all of the races they could handle. Some horses had a lot of stamina, but they also had to be able to handle the sharp turns of the small track. Racing luck was racing luck, so even if you bet with someone on a sure thing, it might not happen! But you had a three day go at it, so there was always next time. It was a lot of excitement for the crowd at Willits.

During the rodeo each day, the Persico family of Willits entertained the rodeo-goers with rope tricks and trick riding. Their oldest son, Lee, who had performed at the 1939 World Fair, was billed as the "World's Youngest Trick Rider", and the audience always enjoyed seeing him perform. This meant that Lee couldn't go goof off with the rest of us kids until after his act. He watched close to see when his time was to go out on the track and do the tricks with his horse. Then, after that was done, he could rip around with us between the carnival and the rodeo grounds. We did check in with our folks once in a while so they knew where to find us. To keep cool all day, we drank lots of cool Orange Crushes. The sweet, wholesome orange taste out of the little brown glass ribbed bottle was unlike any of today's soda pops. Lee Persico, now over sixty, is still rodeoing regulary, but he is not the oldest cowboy, yet!

The whole town of Willits celebrated Frontier Days with decorated windows, various celebration events, parties and get-togethers. It seemed like the town partied all day and all night for a week or more. Some cowboys even rode their horse in through the front door of a saloon to order a drink, saying that there was no place to tie their horse up outside, and they were thirsty. They were served!

Lee Persico Collection

David Bacci Collection

Hotel Willits on Main Street with Doc Babcock's office, upper right building

Hotel Van on the left and Hotel Willits on the right, Main St. left to right

Two of the hotels in town were right across the sidestreet from each other, both on a corner facing Main Street. One was the impressive looking Hotel Willits, where my Grandpa lived, and the other was the Hotel Van. Each was grand in its own way. The Hotel Willits was grand with an Old West flavor.Note the third floor addition in the picture shown on the previous page. It had a fine, well appointed dining room, and a large lobby, and a second story veranda on two sides. The Hotel Van was elegant in a city sort of way, with a marble floored mezzanine furnished with luxurious couches and chairs. It was a brick building, while The Willits Hotel was built of fine woods.

There was not a hotel room in town to be had during the week of July 4th, because we all came in from the ranches and got rooms to stay in town for the whole celebration. The women brought a good supply of homemade food to the rooms with them, so there was never a shortage of something to eat back at your family's room. It was fun to eat with another family, too, to see what kind of treats they had. The carnival was so exciting, so colorfull at night with all the rides and games that we saw only once a year!

At one Rodeo, on a year when my Dad was the Rodeo Chairman, and my Mom was doing rodeo secretary duties in the grandstand, there was an especially exciting event for me. The Montie Montana trick riding family was invited to come and entertain rodeo-goers. Montie's claim to fame was a well done four-horse-catch. I had not seen this done before. In the four-horse-catch, he stood on the ground and threw a large loop around four galloping horses as they passed by him. Not much room for error in this one.

Montie and my Dad were friends. Unknown to me, or my Mom, they had arranged earlier for me to be one of the four riders in that four-horse loop. Montie came up and introduced himself to me as I was watering my horse at the oak tree where he was tied. Montie said he had watched me ride. He asked me if I would like to be in his four-horse-catch, and if I thought my horse and I could do the ride. I was surprised ... all these other good riders around, and he wants me? Eleven year old me? I said I would have to go find my Dad to ask him. Montie said he had already gotten permission from Dad. Montie was short one rider, and the act was going to go on soon.

So I tightened up my cinch, checked my saddle, got on Billy, rode by and caught Dad's eye and got the OK from him. Then I went quickly to do a couple of practice runs with the other three riders to get a feel for staying together in a line across the track with them. Me, riding with the trick riders! I used to pretend to be a trick rider at home on Ridgewood, with my little horse, Billy the Kid, who was very patient with me and my saddle acrobatics as we galloped down one of the lesser used ranch roads. Montie's family and I practiced for a few minutes. Then they signaled that it was time to do it for

Jani Buron Collection

Every Rodeo has flag girls, trick riders, and cowboys

real. They said, "Just ride at an even pace, and when the loop comes over you, just keep going at the same measured pace".

We four started out, stayed even, turned our faces toward the grandstand and smiled at the crowd, and galloped past Montie. He threw a perfect loop around us as we went by. My horse went at just the right speed, and we all four passed through the huge loop Montie had thrown. It was fun! The crowd loved it.

But my Mom didn't know that I was riding in that four-horse-catch until she heard the announcer say, "Here comes Montie Montana's family and Jani Griffith of Willits doing the four-horse-catch!" Dad, who did know, was busy running the Rodeo and hadn't gotten word to her yet, and she was busy with the secretary duties in a front booth in the grandstand. When she heard my name called, she quickly stood up to see if it was really me riding with the group. Her Rodeo secretary papers went flying. She grabbed her camera and clicked it just as a spectator stood up in front of her, and she got a picture of the back of his head, instead of our four-horse-catch! She was so surprised because she didn't know that I was riding in the act, but she was excited and happy! And was I happy! What an adventure.

## BLACK BART ROCK

Black Bart was one of the most notable Northern California bandits of the late 1800's. Part of the lore of Highway 101 near Ridgewood Ranch was the location of Black Bart Rock. The famous rock, named for this legendary man who did business there, was located on the west side of old Highway 101 on a bank just above road level. By the time I was old enough to remember seeing it, there was a low growing tree right next to it that partly covered the rock. It was a round squatty dark rock, wider than it was tall, with a little groove on the top side just large enough to lay a rifle barrel in. Black Bart could stay concealed in back of the rock, and still have his sites on the potential robbery victims. The new highway route built in the 1950's bypasses this spot, and probably few people remember its location and the story that went with it. The rock is no longer there. The Rock became a casualty of modern highway improvement.

Black Bart was a mysterious bandit who made it a point to rob the stages that carried Wells Fargo money. He made it clear that he would not bother the passengers, and that he just wanted the Wells Fargo strongbox. The story goes that he had a bad experience with Wells Fargo in his mining days, and swore to get back what money he had coming to him. He led the double life of a respected citizen and mining engineer living in San Francisco, while at the same time he was robbing stages for about eight years from

Held-Poage House Collection

Black Bart Rock on Hwy 101 just south of Willits, California

1875 to 1883. All that time the law, and Wells Fargo agents were trying to chase him down.

Black Bart, whose real name was Charles E. Boles ( AKA Bowles or Bolton) was a very fit man, and could walk long distances, and did so to get where he was going, because he didn't care for horses. His background of military life and mining prepared him for outdoor living when necessary. He knew the back country of Northern California from previous trips to the area when he had lived back East. From his mining experiences, he was familiar with the stage routes and schedules.

When robbing stages, Black Bart wore the same disguise each time of a flour sack over his head with eye holes cut in it, and a long duster, and sacks on his boots so he wouldn't leave tracks to identify. He was polite in his demands, and did not use foul language. He would sometimes tie long straight sticks to the bushes so they resembled guns of an imaginary gang. He would tell his "gang" to shoot if the driver did not comply and throw down the money box. He himself carried a double barreled shotgun, said to be unloaded.

The posse men that chased him unsuccessfully would go back to the scene of the robbery and look for clues, and often they would find a signed poem written by Black Bart that he left there where they would find it. In spite of the rewards that were being offered for his capture, he had a sense of humor, much to the exasperation of the Wells Fargo investigators who were pursuing him. After robbing a stage, he sometimes would rob the same stage in the same place a day or two later.
One of the more well known Black Bart poems:

*"I've labored long and hard for bread*
*for honor and for riches*
*But on my corns too long you've tred*
*You fine haired Son of Bitches*
*Black Bart*
*the PO 8"*

And another:

*"here I lay me down to sleep*
*to wait the coming morrow*
*perhaps success perhaps defeat*
*and everlasting Sorrow*

*let come what will I'll try it on*
*My condition can't be worse*
*and if theres money in that box*
*'Tis munny in my purse*
*Black Bart*
*the PO 8"*

Black Bart was counted as being responsible for about 28 stage robberies over a period of about eight years. Some of those that took place on the route that went past Ridgewood were:

October 2, 1878, Cahto to Ukiah stage.
October 3, 1878, Covelo to Ukiah.
January 26, 1882, Ukiah to Cloverdale.
June 14, 1882, Little Lake to Ukiah, where Hiram Willits, the Postmaster of Willitsville is a passenger. Willitsville became the town of Willits, as we know it today.

Black Bart's final robbery in November of 1883 was the stage from Sonora to Milton in Calaveras County, where he was slightly injured by a shotgun blast. He used his handkerchief on the wound and then lost it at the scene. His laundry mark of FXO7 was traced to one of the 91 laundries in San Francisco, and he was identified and arrested. What the law officers found was a very proper and polite gentleman, witty in his remarks, and not at all like the wild bandit that some had imagined him to be. He served four years of his six year sentence in San Quentin, and was released on good behavior. He stayed in San Francisco briefly, and then disappeared. There are reports that he was buried in a small town near Sacramento, and also reports that he died in New York in 1917, which would have made him 89 years old. He was a mysterious man, and good at making unexpected appearances, so who knows where he really rests.

## NEW VET QUARTERS and NEW ROUND CORRAL

On the North side of the Upper Mare Barn at Ridgewood Ranch, a small square building next to it served as a breeding shed. It was private, clean, quiet, and offered no distractions. It was a "men only" place, and we children were instructed not to play around there and make loud noises. Of course, when the shed was not occupied, we very quietly approached the mysterious place and peeked in through the crack of the locked door. It looked ordinary to us, just as a working ranch shed should, and so we lost interest in seeing it any further.

Later, that shed was put to a different use, and redesigned and then outfitted with the most modern veterinary equipment we had ever seen. A huge table was in the center, lit up by a very bright overhead light mounted from the central peak in the ceiling. That table could be tipped to different positions, vertical and horizontal, and was made large enough to accommodate a horse so he could easily be examined or x-rayed. The table was put in a vertical position, then the horse was placed next to it, and the restraints were fastened around the horse's body to secure him snugly to the table. He was given a mild sedative to relax him, and then the table scooped him up and presented him to the doctor in a horizontal examining position.

The rest of the room had been outfitted with banks of cabinets and drawers and tables to hold any instruments and medicines that the vet might need. Quite a place. Now, that shed was interesting! We were still told "no admittance" unless some adult was with you. The place had to be kept very clean and orderly. Maybe they had seen what we did years before, the new concoctions we children had mixed up from the old jars of medicines that were on the shelves of the ancient Buggy Horse Barn. We really got quite creative with the various containers of sticky stuff, smelly stuff, and black stuff. We thought it necessary to smear little blobs of these mixtures onto the wooden shelves to see what color it was, and what it would do. What it did in our absence was sit there and become hardened smelly blobs of unidentifiable "stuff" that permanently attached itself to those shelves. Maybe they hadn't noticed that we were more grown-up now and did not do mischief like that any more.

The way the horses that were kept stabled in the Stud Barn got their exercise was usually to be ridden around the ranch on the various dirt roads and trails. They were ridden by exercise boys, and a pony-horse accompanied them to enforce suitable behavior, so they wouldn't get too excitable and injure themselves. The Thoroughbred horses also liked the company of the pony horses. The horses liked this method of exercise because it offered a change of scenery and lots of interesting things to look at. It was good for them because the ground was not always level, and this made them exercise all of their muscles by just walking around.

Then a new round corral was built, which was fine for breaking colts; no corners to get into or to get hurt on, and the high walls of the corral kept their attention on what was going on inside the corral. But I always thought that the older horses, who had once been taken all around the ranch for exercise, did not find the same interest in the corral where they were taken for a measured amount of time doing round and round exercise. They must have missed seeing the changing scenery as they walked along the trails and roads of Ridgewood. Seabiscuit had always enjoyed his outings with Mr. Howard and was so curious about the rest of the animals and people he saw around him. Seabiscuit took in the whole world around him, and seemed to enjoy it all.

Seabiscuit portrait available on canvas 24"x18", by L. Buron. See web site

Seabiscuit portrait, Bay Meadows Handicap 1938, *George Woolf up.* See web site

## LAVERNE'S CHILDHOOD MEMORIES

Looking back on my childhood at Ridgewood Ranch during the "Seabiscuit Years", I realize now this was a very unique experience, enjoyed to the fullest by only a very few fortunate youngsters. My sister, Betty, Jani, and I were outdoor kids, and in our playtime we covered most of the 17,000 acres on foot or on horseback.

I realized Seabiscuit was a famous racehorse, and was somewhat impressed, but I was more interested in the horses I could ride. Mr. Howard was breeding, in addition to the Thoroughbreds, pintos, palominos and other horses for ranch work. My brother Hubert would start the 3-year-olds under saddle, and after a short time he would have me riding them. I remember many adventures over the wonderful trails throughout the ranch with Betty and Jani while I was riding Patches or Jigger or Butterfly or Rosie, or sometimes my own horse, Charro. One time, coming down a steep mountain trail, the colt I was riding bucked me off. As I was getting back on, Jani remarked that I had sailed pretty high through the air! And then we continued on down the trail, ready for the next adventure.

We three girls would spend time now and then at Seabiscuit's barn, watching the visitors come and go. Sometimes I would cut up carrots for Seabiscuit's grain. I have a vivid memory of Seabiscuit standing quietly in his stall, head up and ears forward, his wide-set, intelligent eyes just staring into space. I thought he might be remembering all the races he used to run. Or maybe he was listening for the racetrack bugler's "Call To The Post".

I had been tagging along with my Dad on the morning that we got the sad news that Seabiscuit had died. At the graveside, only a few were there: Mr. Howard, the ranch manager, Dr. John Britton, Seabiscuit's groom, a few ranch hands, my Dad and myself. Everyone was sad and respectfully quiet, but as Mr. Howard turned to walk away he said. "Seabiscuit will show them how to run up in horse heaven."

- Laverne Jones Booth -

## BETTY'S CHILDHOOD MEMORIES

Memories of my childhood living on Ridgewood Ranch brings a smile to my face, remembering the wonderful times with Jani and my sister, Laverne. Because of the great Seabiscuit, my life style was set to always love the outdoors and forever have horses be a part of my life. Even though, at my young age, Seabiscuit was just another ranch horse, I never could understand what all the fuss was about.

Some of my favorite times were the hikes to "Big Rock Candy Mountain". We three girls would pack a lunch, saddle up Doonie, Charro and Billy the Kid and ride to the foot of the mountain where we would tie our horses and begin the steep hike. The excitement of watching for the wild goats, eating our lunch on the summit, and taking the fast way down the shale side of the mountain, wearing out the seat of our pants, these are some of my fondest memories.

Summers were spent cooling off in the lake and creeks and riding bareback through the irrigation sprinklers in the hay fields. My favorite was the creeks. Jani and I would find the deep water holes so we could swim our horses, then on the ride back to the stable, we would detour through the fruit orchards to pick the fresh plums from the trees.

Doonie was my very own pony, however when I went along with my Dad on the cattle and sheep drives, I had the pick of his saddle horses. I rode Blondie, Pal, Tick Tock and Cowboy, my favorite. Daddy said my sister and I were his best hands so we spent many happy days together.

At the bottom of the hill by our house was a big oak tree I loved to climb. My sister and I would wait until the yearling Thoroughbred colts in that pasture would settle down in the shade of that tree and we would slowly slide down on their backs, still holding on to the branches. We got caught one day, by Mr.Howard himself! He told Daddy and that was the end of that. I was so tickled though, to say I rode them first.

Looking back on those days I now realize what a wonderful childhood I had, living in that beautiful country, on that very special ranch, Home of Seabiscuit.

- Betty Jones Peters -

# Chapter 8

## RIDING ALONE: THE GIRLS MOVED AWAY

One day Laverne and Betty came to me and said that they would be moving away soon. Their Dad had found a position he liked on a smaller Northern California ranch, and they would be on Ridgewood for only a few more weeks. We agreed that we would sure all miss each other's company, and our long rides, and the swimming, and so many things. But we would write, and maybe visit now and then, and send pictures to each other. But it would not be the same as it had been at Ridgewood. The Jones girls soon left with their family, and now I was riding alone. I missed their company.

Now that I was riding by myself, my folks changed the ground rules; they wanted to keep a closer tab on where I was riding to, and I was always to be home before dark! And of course, no all-day rides by myself. It wouldn't be any fun anyway, all by myself. Now that I was the only young girl on the ranch, I inherited all the baby sitting jobs for the ranch families, and all the shirt ironing business for the ranch hands. I was the only one going to school from Ridgewood now, so the driver of the town bus and I rode in to school in Willits each week day. I sat in the front seat all the time now, being the only school kid.

The Britton family moved off the ranch next, and the Morgan family moved into their house. The Morgans had three children; the oldest was Hugh, then Tom, in high school, and Betty, about my age. Betty Morgan didn't like to ride as much as the Jones girls had, so I still rode alone a lot.

That year, 1949, was my twelfth summer, and I took a job picking pears in the Howard pear orchard just across the field from our house. Two other older girls and I began picking pears early each morning. For each box you filled, you got 25 cents. There was a pear apron to wear with big pockets to put the pears in as you picked. There was also the bucket method that worked as long as you didn't bruise the pears by putting too many in at one time, and you had to dump them slowly and carefully into the big wooden boxes.

Alameda County Fair Collection

Race track in about 1936. Pleasanton is the oldest race course in the U.S.A.

There was a tall ladder for each of us to use, and we quickly learned to plant the ladder firmly into the plowed ground before climbing it! I got off balance a couple of times while I was near the top of my ladder, and came crashing down, freshly picked pears and all. That was not much fun. I discovered that it sure took a long time to fill a box. It was not as easy money as I thought it would be. Then one day some friends came to visit and wanted to go riding while I was picking pears. The picking was going so slow that I wasn't making much money, and the horseback riding sure sounded good. So I decided to let the pear-picking career go, and left the whole orchard to the other two girls.

## LEAVING RIDGEWOOD

In early Spring of 1950, Mom called me in to the house and told me that we were leaving Ridgewood soon. I was so shocked and surprised, and I needed time to gather my thoughts. I had never thought about leaving this place or living anywhere else. I would sure miss the whole Ranch, and everything on it. "And where were we moving to", I asked? There were a couple of locations that my Dad and Mom were considering. No permanent decisions were made until later that summer.

When we left Ridgewood, Mr. Howard had a parting gift for my Dad. The two men shared a deep love and appreciation of the Thoroughbred horse and horseracing. Mr. Howard gave my Dad one of his fine proven broodmares. Her name was Sag Rock, and she was in foal to Howard's grey stud horse, Sabu, by *Mahmoud. Mr. Howard also said a free breed-back for the following year came with the deal! His generosity was greatly appreciated by my Dad, who had plans to start his own racing stable at the Pleasanton Racetrack when we left Ridgewood. Sag Rock foaled her fine looking little black colt in Willits, and we shipped them to Pleasanton later in the year. The colt turned a pretty silvery-grey color, and his conformation was almost flawless.

In the late Spring of 1950 we moved off the Ranch and into Willits, to a house on Main Street, where we lived for the rest of the summer. At first, I enjoyed the novelty of being a "town girl" and being able to walk to a friend's house, or downtown, or to the movies on my own. But soon that wore thin, and I began to miss the horses and riding and Ridgewood. On an early June day that was the last day of school, my folks threw me a grand surprise combination 13th birthday party and going away party up on the river north of town, and that made for wonderful memories. School chums and teachers and families were there, and we all had a grand day of swimming, roasting hot dogs on a campfire, birthday cake and presents!

"SABU ROCK"
PLEASANTON,CALIF. JULY 1,1957. R.BEASLEY,JOCKEY.
COUSIN SISTER (2nd) 5 ½ fur.1:05 .SCRAPPY DARLIN (3rd)
CHET GRIFFITH,OWNER. NEW TRACK RECORD.CHET GRIFFITH,TRAINER.
7-1-10

Jani Buron Collection

We heard that Mr. Howard's health had continued to deteriorate. He died on June 6th of 1950, leaving behind a massive estate of land ownerships and holdings. There were decisions to be made as to the disposition of it all; what to keep, what to sell. The family and the legal advisors pondered the value of the livestock and the racing stables and the various ranches and homes and other pieces of property Charles and Marcela owned. The question of Ridgewood Ranch came up. Eventually a dispersal sale of some of the Ridgewood Ranch horses, livestock, and equipment was held.

The Fourth of July came around, with the Frontier Days Rodeo and celebration. For the first time we were living in town, within walking distance of all the festivities. That was fun, but it didn't make up for living away from the ranch.

In late August, just one week before school started, it was time to leave, and so we loaded up our four-door Chevy with some of our household goods and clothes and left Willits for Pleasanton, California. Mom drove the car, and Dad drove our horse van with the rest of our belongings packed into it. He left our horses, the mare Sag Rock, who was in foal, and my horse Billy the Kid, in Willits and planned to come back and get them after we got settled in Pleasanton. John, then five years old, was ready to start first grade and I was thirteen and going into high school. Mom had been hired for a teaching job at the Pleasanton Elementary School. Dad would start training horses at the Pleasanton Racetrack.

As Mom was driving the Chevy southbound on Highway 101 out of Willits, I watched from the back window of the car as the well known streets went by, wondering if I would ever see this town or my childhood friends again. As I pondered this, I turned around and sat down in the back seat, looked out the side window, with my attention turning to the familiar roadside scenery south of Willits that was passing by.

We went past the Howard Hospital on the hill; lots of memories there. Then past the familiar homes and ranches of those I knew. Then on toward the hill up to the Forestry. We drove past the Howard Forestry Station, and I was thinking how strange it felt not to stop there, either to see my Grandpa Philbrick, or to get off a school bus and wait there for one of our Moms to come to get us. Then we came to the top of Ridgewood Grade where Big Rock Candy Mountain came in to view. I recalled all the fun times that Laverne, Betty and I had climbing that little mountain. As we traveled on down The Grade, I looked beyond the guardrail at the edge of the highway on down into the Walker Valley and Ridgewood Ranch. I could plainly see all the familiar barns, outbuildings, ranch houses and the hills I had ridden around so often. I looked at Lion Mountain with its heavy growth of fir and pine. I saw the oak woodlands and The Redwood Grove.

The open hay fields and pastures were golden now, in the late Summer. In the Spring, they would be emerald green again. I could see our "new" house on the hill that Mr. Howard had built for us. I missed Ridgewood Ranch already. Would I ever be this way again? Who knows...Good-bye Ridgewood...

Soon we were in less familiar territory, and in an hour or two we were passing through new country. The trip from Willits to Pleasanton took all day, many long hot summer hours, traveling along the two-lane highways and through many towns, large and small.

## NEW TOWN

When we arrived in Pleasanton, the house on the little ranch we had rented in the nearby town of Livermore would not be ready for us to move into until later. The place had a house, a barn, and corrals, and was six miles from Pleasanton. Six miles seemed like a long way then. We could use the barn and corrals, so we put the horses there when Dad brought them down from Willits. Since the house was not yet available, we four moved into an upstairs apartment in The Old Rose Hotel on Main Street in the middle of downtown Pleasanton. School started in a few days, so we quickly unpacked and got as organized as possible. Mom would teach, and John would start first grade at the Pleasanton Elementary school. I would start my freshman year at Amador High School.

School started, and I made a few new friends, usually because of my association with horses. I found that there were students from other racetrack families going to school there at Amador, too, which made it nice. The Pleasanton Racetrack was a new world, an exciting place to be a part of, and I liked helping Dad with the horses. I also liked learning about the Thoroughbred horses at the racetrack that were so different from Thoroughbreds at Ridgewood who were not in training. Seabiscuit had been here in training at the Pleasanton Racetrack in 1936 for a few days when Mr. Howard felt that it was too muddy to train on other California tracks. Seabiscuit had been at this track before me, and had known things about racing that I was just learning. Thoughts of Seabiscuit reminded me about being at Ridgewood, but I knew it was not the same now, anyway, with Mr. Howard being gone.

I liked the small-town atmosphere of Pleasanton; both Pleasanton and Willits had about the same population of just under 2000 when I moved from one town to the other. Pleasanton was a country town with horse ranches and a Thoroughbred racing facility, dairies, cattle operations, and a couple of small cafe's where people met to exchange the daily neighborhood news. The long established Christensen's Tack Room on Main Street had anything needed for livestock tack and doctoring; they also carried Western wear, boots and shoes and clothes. A feed store on Main Street offered sacks of select feeds for livestock, large and small. The small grocery stores located in different neighborhoods across town offered fresh meat and produce and canned goods along with an assortment of sundries. There was a Post Office, one drug store, a small Greyhound Bus depot, one dress shop, a dime store, two doctors, a dentist, a couple of gas stations and an auto repair garage, banks, bars and a pool hall.

The Alameda County Fair was held at the Pleasanton Racetrack and Fair Grounds every year for two weeks in late June, and through July 4th. That was a highlight of the year for the townfolk. Most of the town's population took part in and attended the fair and races, and when the fair was over, most businesses in town closed down for a week or two vacation. The horsemen and their families continued to move on to each county fair in California with racing. It got pretty quiet in Pleasanton while they were gone.

Pleasanton, the oldest racetrack in America, had a long-time reputation of being one of the best racetracks in the country to train horses on. After the County Fair Racing Circuit was over at the end of the summer, the horsemen returned home to Pleasanton where they spent the winter and kept their horses in training at the Pleasanton Racetrack. The racetrack kids went back to school and studied, all the time anticipating the next Spring's preparations for the County Fair Racing Circuit. The fairs were fun, fastpaced, and exciting. During the Winter, some trainers raced their horses at nearby Bay Meadows and Tanforan and Golden Gate Fields. The racetrack of that era is a whole story in itself.

The mare that Mr. Howard gave us took good care of her little grey colt, and he showed fine promise of great early speed. We named him Sabu Rock. His workouts drew attention from other horsemen. When it finally came time for his first race, the anticipation was almost too much to bear. Our own horse, raised from birth that we cared for and trained; we kept him fit and sound, ready to race and watched him for signs of anything that was not quite right. His race day came, we did everything right, all the time wondering what he would do the first time out.

Post time was getting near: Sabu Rock did fine in the paddock and looked ready to run! He looked grand in the post parade; he behaved well in the gate. The starting bell rang, and he broke well. His silvery-grey color made it easy to watch him as he began to lead the pack. He continued to draw out until he won by a 16 length lead at the wire, much to the delight of the cheering Pleasanton racetrack crowd who had been following his workouts. What a breathless happy time for us! A winner the first time out! He paid $16.20 for a $2.00 win ticket that day. His nickname became "The Silver Streak".

He always won his races with fast times, and he set two track records at Pleasanton. He also raced at Tanforan, Bay Meadows, and Golden Gate Fields. He did not race a lot, but he became legendary because of his speed and his silvery-grey appearance as he streaked down the track past horses. Thank you, Mr. Howard. Dad did get two more foals out of Sag Rock, but none compared to Sabu Rock. The dam, Sag Rock, had three foals by Seabiscuit while under Howard ownership. Her 1947 colt, Bart's Rock, was the top money winner of all of Seabiscuit's 108 foals, with $77,883. to his credit.

Ridgewood Ranch was always in the back of my mind, even though I liked being around the horses at the racetrack and working with my Dad. In 1951 the news came that Ridgewood Ranch was sold to the Welch Family of Oregon, who were lumbermen. The Welch Family had several other pieces of property in various locations. They chose Ridgewood as their permanent residence for their main family homes.

The Welches added a new family home near The Big House. They also made some changes in The Big House, and installed some major farm equipment down at the ranch main headquarters. They logged some of the timber, but left the Redwood trees. They built a lumber mill across Highway 101 from the main ranch gate, and shipped their products out of that location. They kept Ridgewood as a working cattle ranch also. They maintained the property well, and enjoyed living there, as had all those that lived there before them.

The next, and current, owner of Ridgewood Ranch became Christ's Church of The Golden Rule, who purchased it from the Welch Brothers in 1962. At the time of purchase, the working livestock part of the ranch remained much the same as it had when the Welches bought it from the Howard family. The Church members are focused on keeping it a working cattle ranch, while restoring what remains of this historical site, and opening it to the public periodically for tours, and to youth programs and other beneficial projects. With the help of the community and many other supporters, this is being done very effectively. Ridgewood Ranch has recently been designated as a historical landmark, and with community help, the barns and other buildings are being restored.

# Epilogue

## THE END OF THE STORY: OR IS IT?

In 1954 I graduated from Amador High School in Pleasanton, California, and in my four years here in a racetrack town, I had learned a lot more about racehorses and racing. Seabiscuit's name came up quite often in the discussion of great horses of the day. He was still America's hero, even with many other great horses who were now making a name for themselves.

In the margins of my highschool homework papers, and on the edges of my college art easel board, I doodled the Ridgewood Ranch Triangle "H" brand used on the stall doors and the Howard racing silks, and the Quarter Circle "H" brand used on Ridgewood livestock. It seemed to keep me connected with that very happy time in my life when I lived at Ridgewood Ranch.

Whenever a discussion came up about who was the greatest racehorse of all time, that is, the fastest running, the most thrilling to ride, the biggest heart, the most courageous, the most intelligent, and the most notable for his achievements against all odds, I always explained that Seabiscuit was most worthy of this honor. I had admired and learned about many great racehorses, famous and otherwise, but The Biscuit always stood out as my favorite. Seabiscuit always gave it all he had, and then some. His great heart and his superior horse intelligence and his kind ways are some of his greatest attributes. Besides all that, I knew him personally! As far as being memorable for going above and beyond his expectations, Seabiscuit was always lengths ahead of the field in my book!

With the returning popularity of the timeless Seabiscuit story, and the release of my book, "Ridgewood Ranch, Home of Seabiscuit", I have had many new contacts, personal appearances, media appearances, interviews, booksignings, a surprising amount of fan mail, Email, personal letters, gifts and the most heartwarming of all, the many wonderful people who have shared their special stories and thoughts about Seabiscuit, horseracing, the Howards and Ridgewood. All of you have helped make this book possible. This keeps the Spirit of Seabiscuit alive! I accepted the invitation to return to Ridgewood Ranch as a storyteller for the guests at the popular summer walking tours. I do booksigning there, too. I have met many enthusiastic guests who visited Ridgewood Ranch and enjoyed the unique experience of seeing Seabiscuit's home first hand.

In the racing records that follow you will find a lot of names and numbers, all statistical information. Those names and numbers remind Laverne, Betty and Jani of seeing the frisky little un-named foals running in circles around their Mamas in the paddocks out in the sunshine. We looked over each crop of babies and picked out our favorites. We each had our favorite mares and watched them from year to year to check out their new babies. Their names roll off our tongues, even now, as we remember them at Ridgewood ... Illeana, Grey Nurse, Chiquita Mia, Carmanchita, Lucille K., Dark Convent, Sag Rock ... and more.

Jani Buron Collection

Laverne, Jani and Betty back at Ridgewood after 52 years

SEABISCUIT
AND
HIS FIRST THREE WINNERS 1943

Jani Buron Collection

# Seabiscuit's Offspring
and
# Racing Records

Bay Horse - foaled 1933 in Kentucky at the Claiborne Farms
Breeder: Wheatley Stables

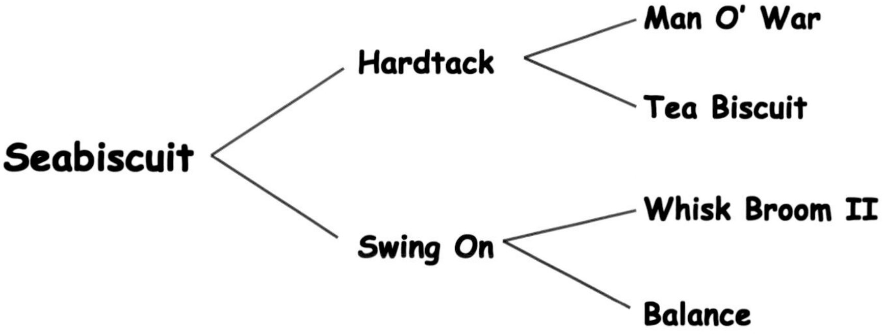


Racing Record USA and Canada

| | starts | 1st | 2nd | 3rd |
|---|---|---|---|---|
| Total Races | 89 | 33 | 15 | 13 |
| Stakes & Handicap | | 26 | 7 | 6 |

| YEAR | AGE | STARTS | EARNINGS | 1ST | 2ND | 3RD |
|---|---|---|---|---|---|---|
| 1935 | 2 | 35 | 12,500 | 5 | 7 | 5 |
| 1936 | 3 | 23 | 28,995 | 9 | 1 | 5 |
| 1937 | 4 | 15 | 168,395 | 11 | 2 | 1 |
| 1938 | 5 | 11 | 130,395 | 6 | 4 | 1 |
| 1939 | 6 | 1 | 400 | 0 | 1 | 0 |
| 1940 | 7 | 4 | 96,850 | 2 | 0 | 1 |
| | | TOTAL | **$437,730.00** | | | |

| | | |
|---|---|---|
| 1937 | USA | Champion Handicap Horse |
| 1938 | USA | Horse of the Year |
| 1938 | USA | Champion Handicap Horse |
| 1938 | USA | Pimlico Special ( MATCH RACE ) |

**A very well-centered horse with a spectacular racing career**

# Handicap Racing Record

**Seabiscuit 1938 set new track record 1 3/16 mi. in 1:56.60 at Pimlico**

| Year | Place | Country | Race | Purse |
|---|---|---|---|---|
| 1935 | 1 | USA | Ardsley Handicap | 2,500 |
| 1935 | 1 | USA | Springfield Handicap | 2,500 |
| 1935 | 1 | USA | Watch Hill Claming Stakes | 2,500 |
| 1936 | 1 | USA | Mohawk Claming stakes | 2,000 |
| 1936 | 1 | USA | Hendrie Handicap | 2,500 |
| 1936 | 1 | USA | Bay Bridge Handicap | 2,500 |
| 1936 | 1 | USA | Scarsdale Handicap | 5,000 |
| 1936 | 1 | USA | Worlds Fair Handicap | 10,000 |
| 1936 | 1 | USA | Governors Handicap | 5,000 |
| 1937 | 1 | USA | Laurel Stakes | 7,500 |
| 1937 | 1 | USA | Yonkers Handicap | 7,500 |
| 1937 | 1 | USA | Riggs Handicap | 10,000 |
| 1937 | 1 | USA | Marchbank Handicap | 10,000 |
| 1937 | 1 | USA | Bay Meadows Handicap | 10,000 |
| 1937 | 1 | USA | San Jaun Capistrano Handicap | 10,000 |
| 1937 | 1 | USA | Butler Handicap | 20,000 |
| 1937 | 1 | USA | Brooklyn Handicap | 20,000 |
| 1937 | 1 | USA | *Massachusetts Handicap | 50,000 |
| 1937 | 1 | USA | Continental Handicap | 10,000 |
| 1938 | 1 | USA | Havre De Grace Handicap | 10,000 |
| 1938 | 1 | USA | Agua Caliente Handicap | 12,500 |
| 1938 | 1 | USA | Bay Meadows Handicap | 15,000 |
| 1938 | 1 | USA | *Hollywood Gold Cup | 50,000 |
| 1940 | 1 | USA | San Antonio Handicap | 10,000 |
| 1940 | 1 | USA | **Santa Anita Handicap | 100,000 |
| 1935 | 2 | USA | Pawtucket Handicap | 5,000 |
| 1937 | 2 | USA | Bowie Handicap | 10,000 |
| 1937 | 2 | USA | **Santa Anita Handicap | 100,000 |
| 1938 | 2 | USA | Laurel Stakes | 7,500 |
| 1938 | 2 | USA | San Antonio Handicap | 7,500 |
| 1938 | 2 | USA | Stars and Stripes Handicap | 10,000 |
| 1938 | 2 | USA | **Santa Anita Handicap | 100,000 |
| 1935 | 3 | USA | Juvenile Handicap | 5,000 |
| 1936 | 3 | USA | East Hills Handicap | 2,500 |
| 1936 | 3 | USA | Western Hills Handicap | 2,500 |
| 1936 | 3 | USA | Yorktown Handicap | 5,000 |
| 1937 | 3 | USA | Narragansett Special Handicap | 25,000 |
| 1938 | 3 | USA | Manhattan Handicap | 5,000 |

* $50,000 purses ** $100,000 purses

# Seabiscuit's Offspring

There were 108 sired, 50 colts - 58 fillies
Breeding Seasons from 1939 to 1947

| FOAL | YEAR | COLOR/SEX | OUT OF | DAM BY | EARNINGS |
|---|---|---|---|---|---|
| Sea Belle | 1940 | b F | - Flying Belle | by Flying Ebony | Unraced |
| Sea Convoy | 1940 | ch G | - Illeanna | by Polymelian | 9,930 |
| Sea Frolic | 1940 | b F | - Sun Frolic | by Sun Briar | 12,000 |
| Sea Night | 1940 | b C | - Fair Knightness | by Bright Knight | 0 |
| Sea Mite | 1940 | ch F | - Dressage | by Bull Dog | Unraced |
| Sea Patrol | 1940 | br G | -Lady Riaf | by War Cry | 2,175 |
| Sea Skipper | 1940 | b G | - Lucille K. | by Whiskalong | 3,443 |
| Dressed Up | 1941 | b F | - Dressage | by Bull Dog | 1,800 |
| Sea Anemone | 1941 | ch F | - Lucille K. | by Whiskalong | Unraced |
| Tea and Cakes | 1941 | b F | - Pusilla | by Dastur | Unraced |
| Bismarck Sea | 1942 | ch C | - Frivolous III | by Coronach | 30,430 |
| Conning Tower | 1942 | b F | - Fair Margaret | by Fairway | Unraced |
| General's Aide | 1942 | b C | - Jennie Gal | by Sir Gallahad III | 19,780 |
| Mediterranrean | 1942 | br C | - Dark Convent | by Traumer | 35,635 |
| Paramarine | 1942 | b C | - Carmanchita | by Sickle | 19,794 |
| Phantom Sea | 1942 | b C | - Fair Knightess | by BrightKnight | 67,627 |
| Sand Castle | 1942 | b F | - Flying Sands II | by Sandwich | 0 |
| Sea Aide | 1942 | br F | - Grey Nurse | by Sir Greysteel | 295 |
| Sea Floe | 1942 | b F | - Flo II | by Alcantara II | 4,880 |
| Sea Gnat | 1942 | b F | - Black Gnat | by Chicle | Unraced |
| Sea Isle | 1942 | b F | - Sonja II | by Santiago | 4,090 |
| Sea Kit | 1942 | br F | - Catherine Glover | by Gainsborough | 0 |
| Sea Lion | 1942 | b C | - Coramine | by Stimulus | 9,922 |
| Sea Lullaby | 1942 | ch F | - Star Singer | by Caruso | 5,896 |
| Sea Nymph | 1942 | b F | - Ice Maiden | by Buchan | Unraced |
| Sea Sovereign | 1942 | b C | - Queen Helen | by Light Brigade | 34,070 |
| Sea Spray | 1942 | b F | - Sun Frolic | by Sun Briar | 61,085 |
| Sea Swallow | 1942 | br C | - Illeanna | by Polymelian | 61,869 |
| Sea Virgin | 1942 | ch F | - Virginia II | by Gainsborough | 0 |

# Seabiscuit's Offspring

There were 108 sired, 50 colts - 58 fillies
Breeding Seasons from 1939 to 1947

| FOAL | YEAR | COLOR/SEX | OUT OF DAM BY | EARNINGS |
|---|---|---|---|---|
| Sea Warrior | 1942 | h C | Joan Orpen by Orpen | 9,295 |
| Arabian Sea | 1943 | b C | Golden Araby by Golden Sun | 4,175 |
| King Biscuit | 1943 | b C | Liberte III by Tresiete | Unraced |
| Queen Biscuit | 1943 | ch F | Frivolous by Coronach | 2,725 |
| Sea Ace | 1943 | b C | Carmanchita by Sickle | 1,215 |
| Sea Fiddler | 1943 | ch C | Virginia II by Gainsborough | 4,984 |
| Sea Flyer | 1943 | b C | Flying Sands II by Sandwich | 14,182 |
| Sea Goddess | 1943 | b F | Catherine Glover by Gainsborough | 2,231 |
| Sea Imp | 1943 | b F | Buskin by Blandford | 5 ,315 |
| Sea Knightess | 1943 | ch F | Fair Knightess by Bright Knight | 0 |
| Sea Maid | 1943 | br F | Nedtica by Neddie | 0 |
| Sea Queen | 1943 | br F | Fishwife by Halcyon | 500 |
| Sea Vista | 1943 | br F | Sag Rock, by Rock Man | 1,605 |
| Super Bomber | 1943 | ch C | Lucille K. by Whiskalong | 20,740 |
| Caspian Sea | 1944 | ch C | Gay Knightess by Bright Knight | 33,485 |
| Mia Mar | 1944 | br F | Chiquita Mia by Hadagal | 150 |
| Sea Action | 1944 | b C | Fair Knightness by Bright Knight | 0 |
| Sea Flasher | 1944 | b C | Illeanna by Polymelian | 9,564 |
| Sea Food | 1944 | br F | Fishwife by Halcyon | Unraced |
| Sea Glory | 1944 | ch F | Virginia II by Gainsborough | 10,025 |
| Sea Gold | 1944 | gr F | Goldrim by Tetratema | 2,900 |
| Sea Image | 1944 | ch F | Fair Margaret by Fairway | 150 |
| Sea Liberty | 1944 | b F | Liberte III by Tresiete | Unraced |
| Sea Prince | 1944 | b C | Queen Helen by Light Brigade | 1,270 |
| Sea Quest | 1944 | br F | Black Gnat by Chicle | 0 |
| Sea Ruler | 1944 | br C | Dark Convent by Traumer | 1,095 |
| Sea Song | 1944 | ch F | Sonja II by Santiago | 31,069 |
| Sea Spoils | 1944 | ch F | Frivolous by Coronach | Unraced |
| Sea Tide | 1944 | br F | Joan Orpen by Orpen | 0 |

# Seabiscuit's Offspring

There were 108 sired, 50 colts - 58 fillies

Breeding Seasons from 1939 to 1947

| FOAL | YEAR | COLOR/SEX | OUT OF | DAM BY | EARNINGS |
|---|---|---|---|---|---|
| Sea Wave | 1944 | b F | Miss Yankee | by Bostonian | unraced |
| Sparkling Sea | 1944 | b C | Marie Galante | by Brantome | 1,210 |
| Tropical Sea | 1944 | b C | Dreamland | by Chicle | 64,665 |
| Flying Clipper | 1945 | b C | Carmanchita | by Sickle | 1,305 |
| Gay Biscuit | 1945 | b C | Gay Knightess | by Bright Knight | 8,037 |
| Sea Angel | 1945 | ch F | Flo II | by Alcantara II | 22,215 |
| Sea Clipper | 1945 | ch C | Illeanna | by Polymelian | 8,980 |
| Sea Countess | 1945 | b F | Fair Knightess | by BrightKnight | 20,155 |
| Sea Going | 1945 | ch C | Dreamland | by Chicle | 11,320 |
| Sea Majesty | 1945 | b C | Queen Helen | by Light Brigade | 0 |
| Sea Nun | 1945 | br F | Dark Convent | by Traumer | unraced |
| Sea Officer | 1945 | ch C | Frivolous III | by Coronach | 680 |
| Sea Splendor | 1945 | ch C | Sun Frolic | by Sun Briar | 17,145 |
| Sea Sturgeon | 1945 | br C | Fishwife | by Halcyon | 5,882 |
| Sea Treasure | 1945 | b F | Goldrim | by Tetratema | 4,515 |
| Seagaret | 1945 | ch F | Fair Margaret | by Fairway | unraced |
| Miss Veloz | 1946 | b F | Yolandita | by Snark | 1,340 |
| My Biscuit | 1946 | ch F | Seventh Heaven | by Hustle On | 460 |
| Rice Biscuit | 1946 | br F | Rice Crop | by Sickle | 775 |
| Sea Beauty | 1946 | ch F | Illeanna | by Polymelian | 3,410 |
| Sea Crag | 1946 | ch C | Sag Rock | by Rock Man | unraced |
| Sea Flight | 1946 | b C | Flying Sands II | by Sandwich | unraced |
| Sea Linn | 1946 | ch C | Chiquita Mia | by Hadagal | unraced |
| Sea Monarch | 1946 | b C | Fair Knightess | by Bright Knight | 6,970 |
| Sea Sister | 1946 | ch F | Dark Convent | by Traumer | unraced |
| Sea Voyager | 1946 | b C | Frivolous III | by Coronach | 0 |
| Super Sea | 1946 | br C | Carmanchita | by Sickle | 5,595 |
| Bart's Rock** | 1947 | b C | Sag Rock | by Rock Man | 77,883 |
| Embarcadero | 1947 | b F | Boston Lu | by Bostonian | 485 |

** Highest money winning colt by Seabiscuit

** Highest money winning colt by Seabiscuit

# Seabiscuit's Offspring

There were 108 sired, 50 colts - 58 fillies

Breeding Seasons from 1939 to 1947

| FOAL | YEAR | COLOR | SEX | OUT OF DAM BY | EARNINGS |
|---|---|---|---|---|---|
| Gala Sea | 1947 | b | C | - Galomar by Sir Gallahad III | 875 |
| My Sea | 1947 | br | C | - Chiquita Mia by Hadagal | 8,515 |
| Sea Comber | 1947 | b | C | - Sonja II by Santiago | 60 |
| Sea Consort | 1947 | br | F | - Queen Helen by Light Brigade | 1,450 |
| Sea Dreamer | 1947 | br | C | - Dreamland by Chicle | 41,250 |
| Sea Galley | 1947 | ch | F | - Alahad by Sir Gallahad III | 4,962 |
| Sea Gambol | 1947 | b | C | - Sun Frolic by Sun Briar | 70,750 |
| Sea Garden | 1947 | b | F | - Illeanna by Polymelian | 42,450 |
| Sea Mate | 1947 | b | C | - Buskin by Blanford | 425 |
| Sea Mine | 1947 | b | F | - Coramine by Stimulus | 520 |
| Sea Novice | 1947 | b | F | - Dark Convent by Traumer | 14,300 |
| Sea Pilgrim | 1947 | b | F | - Salem Skirt by By-Pass II | 662 |
| Sea Trader | 1947 | b | C | - Alaska Queen by Kayak II | 11,905 |
| Seabehest | 1947 | b | F | - Behest by Blue Larkspur | 5,407 |
| Disentangle | 1948 | b | F | - Revelled by Soon Over | Unraced |
| Sea Flora | 1948 | ch | F | - Illeanna by Polymelian | 6,255 |
| Sea Memory | 1948 | br | F | - Galomar by Sir Gallahad III | 1,905 |
| Sea Mistress | 1948 | b | F | - Fair Knightess by Bright Knight | 5,475 |
| Sea Scholar | 1948 | b | C | - Alma Mater by Rhodes Scholar | 10,298 |
| Sea Vengence | 1948 | b | C | - Flying Sands II by Sandwich | 10,773 |
| Shady Biscuit | 1948 | ch | F | - All Forlorn by Menifee | 0 |

All of Seabiscuit's 108 foals combined earned $ 1,043,465

**THE SPIRIT LIVES ON**

# Acknowledgements

*Many people are a part of this book; their support and assistance is what made it possible. Many thanks go to:*

The Howard family members for their interest and their gracious contribution of time, information, photographs, and leads; Barbara B. Howard, Chuck and Michele Howard, Col. Michael and Lynn Howard, and all the family. We appreciate having the use of the Howard family photos and movie film that was so carefully kept through so many years.

Lee and Evelyn Persico and the entire Persico Family for their continual help and support and encouragement, and for inviting us to stay on their P/6 Ranch in Willits, where much of this book was written. They also supplied important Willits Frontier Days and Rodeo historical information along with photos and memorabelia. Thanks to Evelyn for urging me to go back to Ridgewood for a long overdue visit on that day in late December of 2001. I had not been back since we left in 1950. That visit rekindled many memories.

The Jones Family, Laverne Jones Booth and Betty Jones Peters, for being there, and for their interest and encouragement, and for the use of their old family photographs, and their own stories. Thanks Terry Tours for your family photo and comments of Frank Tours accomplishments.

Louise Rodrigue of Ukiah for the very special 1939 picture taken by her husband, Leland, at age 14 when he visited Ridgewood Ranch; the photo is of Seabiscuit, with Red Pollard up, and Tick Tock is beside him. She brought the photo to me, and told me the story that went with it.

John Bosko, for the generous use of pictures from his great private collection of Seabiscuit-Howard-Ridgewood. Kay Dee Reynolds was the photographer of some of the photos in the John Boskos collection

Robert and Lila Lee of the Held-Poage House and Mendocino County Historical Society in Ukiah for historical information and photos, and encouragement to "get that history written!"

David "Fritz" Bacci of Willits who offered the use of photos from his great files of Mendocino County history.

To Joe and Peggy Ferguson, in memoriam, and daughter Betty Jo for the photos with Joe up on Seabiscuit. In 1938 Joe also galloped and worked Ligaroti when they were on the west coast. Nearing the Seabiscuit-Ligaroti match race Joe favored Seabiscuit. Joe Ferguson later became a race track steward in California.

Bill and Linda Meyerhoff of Willits who loaned their inherited collection of photos of early Ridgewood Ranch days from their friend, Fred Finke.

Jann Lamprich, Administrator of the Frank R. Howard Foundation, for the photos and particular facts about Howard Hospital history and Doc Babcock.

Martha Mitchell, descendant of the Angle Family, for her gracious help in relating the family story to me, which I had been curious about since I lived on Ridgewood as a child, and had seen the Angle names in their family cemetery we visited. Martha provided me with their family tree and special photos.

Annette Deghi Hicks, a classmate, for her family memories and their Howard connection during the World War II years in Willits; Joan Petty, also a classmate, for her photo and input.

The Barn Builders of that day for their stories, Sully Pinches and George Recagno; Floyd Banker for his account of Mr. Howard's gift of their Ukiah house; Eddie Murphy (103!) of Elko for his "new automobile" story, and for a delightful visit.

Gary Welch and the Welch Family for taking the time to fill me in on their years of Ridgewood ownership and their fond memories of living there.

The Recorders Office in Elko, Nevada, where Renee Wright helped us locate the information we needed to begin our search on "The Elko Connection"; and Dottie Gleason of Sparks, Nevada, who was there at the time, and had important leads for us.

The ladies who made us feel so welcome at the Northeastern Nevada Museum in Elko, Nevada, Cheryl Carpenter, Archives Assistant, and Marilyn Pennington, Archivist, for the gracious sharing of their historical ranching folders, newspaper files, photos, information, and leads to Elko citizens who were part of The Elko Connection. All of those gentlemen had such interesting horseracing stories to relate.

Foreman, Jon Griggs, and office manager, Susan Davis of the Maggie Creek Ranch in Elko, Nevada, for the historical information they supplied on the ranch that C. S. Howard once owned.

The Jockey Club Information System Inc. of Lexington, Kentucky, who provided accurate and complete Seabiscuit Handicap records and foal information. A vast amount of information can be located through their Website www.equineline.com

To Bay Meadows, Del Mar Thoroughbred Club, Golden Gate Fields, Oak Tree Racing, Pimlico Race Course and Santa Anita Park managements for their support and encouragement to us.

... With special thanks to Nancy Wallen, Santa Anita Horsemens Liaison Racing Office Secretary, for assistance and personal support throught the writing of this book.

To Alameda County Fair Association, Del Mar Thoroughbred Club, Oak Tree Racing, Pimlico Race Course, Santa Anita Park, for the use of historic racetrack photos and film.

To Christ's Church of The Golden Rule for hosting the Ridgewood Ranch Walking Tours of 2002, 2003, 2004, and 2005, and to everyone at Ridgewood for the gracious hospitality they have extended to us and to the Seabiscuit public.

To my many readers who came forward with their own Seabiscuit-Howard-Racetrack stories that added so much interest. The "Seabisuit Orange Crate" lady from Southern California whose father took an extra job to earn enough money to buy a radio so they could listen to Seabiscuit's races, and her Mom sewed her a little set of Howard red and white racing silks that she wore on "Seabiscuit" days; those people who told of seeing Seabiscuit's rail car coming through town and they caught a glimpse of him; a lady at Bay Meadows who told me that her Grandfather got her out of school one day so they could go see The Biscuit run, and she still has the racing program; a lady who said she and her husband had gone to see Seabiscuit race at Bay Meadows, and she said, "That horse (Seabiscuit) will win", and he said "NO, not that one" and he bet on another horse (guess who was right!); Steve Smith, who shared such special items with us as he added them to his Seabiscuit memorabilia collection; and to Chris Lowe who shared his special collection and information with us.

To Evelyn Persico and Erni Porro for their years of help and support at my book signings, and for their personal attention to anything that was needed.

To my Mother Inez Griffith for getting me a camera years ago and for her taking some of the pictures then, that are so fitting now to share with all of you.

To my husband and partner, Vic Buron, who with his editing and graphic skills so expertly placed pages and pictures in this book, created the great cover design, and guided me through times when my computer would suddenly glitch in mid-story, causing near panic to this writer.

To my wonderful, thorough proof readers with the good eyes who must read through the stuff and pick up on errors, and make suggestions on what might make it a better story; Lynn Schulz, Vicki Beaupre, Evelyn Persico, Laverne Booth, Michele Howard and Barbara B. Howard.

# The End

# Index of Photos

## Index of Photos

L. L. Publishing P.O. Box 12 Wellington, Nevada 89444

***Ordering information** and **other items***
***on our***
***web pages***

**www.janiburon.com**
**or**
**www.thespiritofseabiscuit.com**

A *DVD* supplement

ISBN 0-9720755-2-6
ISBN 978-0-9720755-2-7 BOOK
LCCN 2005902360

DVD ISBN 0-9720755-4-2

## Other Books by Jani Buron:

*RIDGEWOOD RANCH, HOME OF SEABISCUIT*
Author <> Jani Buron
Photos <> Jani Buron

ISBN 0-9720755-0-X

*THE MAYFLOWER TO MENDOCINO*
Written and Compiled <> Jani Buron

ISBN 0-9720755-1-8

*JANI'S FAVORITE WILDGAME RECIPES*
Published on CD Rom
Author <> Jani Buron
Illustrations <> Jani Buron

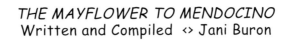

0 33131 54545 4

*RUBEZAHL, THE ADVENTUROUS MOUNTAIN SPIRIT*
Author <> Piri Korngold Nesselrod
Illustrations and book jacket <> Jani Buron

ISBN 0-533-12490-5